THE Aftermath OF THE
Russian Revolution

KATHLYN GAY

 Twenty-First Century Books MINNEAPOLIS

Twenty-First Century Books
A division of Lerner Publishing Group, Inc.
241 First Avenue North
Minneapolis, MN 55401 U.S.A.

Website address: www.lernerbooks.com

Consultant: Paula Ramaley, former director of the Fulbright Fund in Moscow

Library of Congress Cataloging-in-Publication Data

Gay, Kathlyn.
    The aftermath of the Russian Revolution / by Kathlyn Gay.
        p.   cm. — (Aftermath of history)
    Includes bibliographical references and index.
    ISBN 978-0-8225-9092-7 (lib. bdg. : alk. paper)
    1. Soviet Union—History—Juvenile literature. I. Title.
DK266.G29 2009
947.084—dc22   2008025276

Manufactured in the United States of America
1 2 3 4 5 6 – BP – 14 13 12 11 10 09

Contents

Disorder and Rebellion

THE WINTER OF 1917 was bitter cold in Russia. In the capital city of Petrograd (present-day Saint Petersburg) in northwestern Russia, streets were covered with ice. Trains with carloads of grain headed for Petrograd were stuck in snow piled high on tracks.

Shivering women and children stood in long lines for hours waiting to buy bread. But the bakeries had no flour for bread and no fuel for baking, and shelves were bare. People had to return empty-handed to their homes, where there was little or no heat. Even when wood or coal was available, the poor had no money to buy it. People all over Petrograd, with a population of 2.5 million, were incensed over the shortages of basic necessities. These shortages were due in part to Russia's long and costly involvement in World War I (1914–1918).

Three years earlier, Britain and France joined Russia as the Allies in fighting against the Central Powers—Germany and Austria-

Hungary, Turkey, and Bulgaria. Russian armies suffered huge losses. Between 1914 and 1917, 1.7 million Russian soldiers died and almost 5 million were wounded. Another 2.4 million were captured by the Germans.

In the summer of 1915, there were so many Russian defeats in battle that Nicholas II, Russia's czar (emperor), went to the front to take control of the army. Most of the soldiers were young peasants— poor farmers—drafted into the military. They were not well trained and had inadequate equipment. Frequently, the army was forced to retreat. By the end of 1916, Russian workers and peasants were reaching the point of revolt. Their children were the ones being killed in the war, while those at home were hungry and cold.

A Vast Empire

IN THE EARLY 1900s, the Russian Empire covered one-sixth of Earth's land area, stretching across eastern Europe and Asia. People of diverse cultures and national backgrounds lived in the various regions. German farmers, for example, had settled along the Volga River and had become prosperous. Buddhist nomads lived in tents in the eastern part of the empire. Russian Cossacks lived in villages north of the Caucasus and the Black Sea and seldom allowed any other groups to become part of their communities. In the mountain areas of the Caucasus, shepherds roamed.

In the twenty-first century, more than one hundred minority languages are spoken in Russia. Russian is the state language, however, and it is used by about 81 percent of a population estimated at more than 141 million.

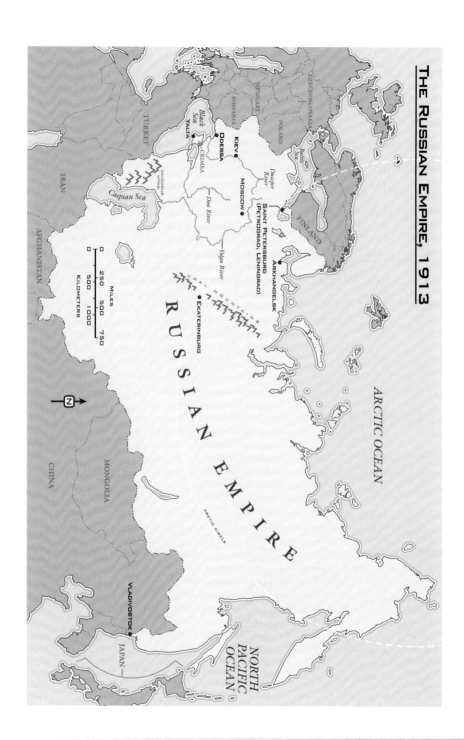

THE RUSSIAN EMPIRE, 1913

TURKEY

Black Sea
YALTA
CRIMEA
ODESSA
KIEV
MOSCOW
Dnieper River
Don River
SAINT PETERSBURG
(PETROGRAD, LENINGRAD)
ARKHANGELSK
Volga River
URAL MOUNTAINS
EKATERINBURG
CAUCASUS MTNS.
Caspian Sea
IRAN
AFGHANISTAN

ROMANIA
HUNGARY
CZECHOSLOVAKIA
POLAND
Baltic Sea
FINLAND

RUSSIAN EMPIRE

ARCTIC OCEAN

ARCTIC CIRCLE

CHINA
MONGOLIA

VLADIVOSTOK
JAPAN

NORTH PACIFIC OCEAN

N

MILES
0   250   500
KILOMETERS
0   500   1000   750

Blaming the Czar

People blamed Nicholas II and his wife, Alexandra, for their problems. Nicholas was a member of the Romanov family, a monarchy that had ruled Russia since 1613. The czar had absolute power, and people had no say in his decisions.

On February 17, 1917, workers in Petrograd, who barely made enough money to survive, began a strike for better wages. They also were protesting the lack of food and fuel. Five days later, on February 22, huge crowds gathered in Petrograd streets. Protestors, including activists of the Bolshevik Party (a workers' political party that called for the overthrow of the czar), carried red banners with slogans such as "Down with the War!" and "Down with the Czar!"

WORKERS DEMONSTRATE ON THE STREETS OF PETROGRAD DURING THE FEBRUARY REVOLUTION IN 1917.

Calendar Differences

IN DISCUSSIONS ABOUT THE 1917 uprising in Petrograd, some history books use a date in early March 1917, rather than February 22. The dates depend on which calendar is used. Russians under the czar followed the Julian calendar of the Russian Orthodox Church. Called the Old Style calendar, it was thirteen days behind the Gregorian calendar used in Western Europe. Russia adopted the Gregorian (New Style) calendar in 1918.

One witness to the demonstrations on February 22 was Ekaterina Olitskaia. She was a student at a women's agricultural institute in Petrograd, and she was on her way to the institute when Cossacks, wearing black capes and hats, appeared on horseback. The Cossacks were members of an imperial army unit. As Olitskaia reported:

> They came riding straight for the demonstrators with their whips raised high in the air. . . . The Cossack detachment cut into the crowd. The crowd parted and pressed up against the buildings on either side. Then I heard a loud "Hurrah!". . . Restraining their horses and still holding their whips high in the air, the Cossacks rode through the middle of the crowd . . . [then] disappeared.

Though stunned at first, the demonstrators realized that this Cossack army unit had joined with them, even though other such regiments were loyal to the czar. People began crying, hugging each other, and cheering even more. They were convinced that a revolution had begun.

CHAPTER 1

From the February Days to a Military Coup

THE REVOLUTION THAT BEGAN in Petrograd in late February lasted only a short time—into the first week of March 1917. Frequently the time period has been called the February Days, Glorious February, or the February Revolution.

During that last week in February 1917, strikes closed down nearly all factories, shops, stores, and businesses in Petrograd. Streetcars no longer ran. Posters on walls and fences urged people to rise up against the czar.

February 23 was International Women's Day, a holiday to honor the struggles of working women. It was not a day marked for strikes, but female textile workers in Petrograd left their jobs to march. The weather had moderated somewhat, and under a bright, sunny sky, the striking women called for "bread and peace." Male factory workers soon joined them.

The czar had gone to army headquarters in Mogilev, along the Russian border with Belarus in eastern Europe. He had been assured by a few of his ministers (government officials) that the protests in the capital would end soon. His wife, Czarina Alexandra, who was in Petrograd, was equally optimistic. She sent Nicholas a report about the worker demonstrations, noting that they were nothing but a "hooligan movement"—rowdy youths trying to "create excitement, along with the workers who prevent others from working. If the weather were very cold they would probably all stay home."

Officials of the Duma, the Russian legislature, became increasingly concerned, however. They sent a telegram to the czar warning, "Situation serious. Anarchy [lawlessness] in the capital. Government paralyzed."

"SECOND BLOODY SUNDAY"

By February 25, up to two hundred thousand workers were in the streets protesting. On February 26, a Sunday, Petrograd's military commander sent troops to break up the crowds. For a short time, the streets were relatively quiet, but in the afternoon, crowds began to gather again. Police and soldiers shot some marchers. During a political rally at Znamenskaya Square on the Nevsky Prospekt, a main thoroughfare in Petrograd, people defied soldiers' orders to leave. Troops firing on the crowd killed fifty people.

The violent incident sparked angry protests among workers. Some workers went to headquarters of military regiments in the city to report that soldiers had killed civilians. They called the massacre the second Bloody Sunday. The first Bloody Sunday had been a 1905 incident in which palace guards shot hundreds of peaceful workers who were demonstrating before the czar's Winter Palace in St. Petersburg.

Bloody Sunday, 1905

IN 1905 CZAR NICHOLAS II was not a popular emperor. He had made no effort to change the repressive policies of his father. In addition, there was industrial unrest. Russian workers labored twelve to sixteen hours six days a week in crowded, unsanitary factories for little pay. On January 9, 1905, impoverished workers from various parts of the city marched to the Winter Palace in St. Petersburg (as it was called before 1914. After 1924, the city was known as Leningrad). The workers hoped to convince Nicholas II that labor reforms were needed. They also wanted the czar to allow the election of members of the legislature.

At the palace, the workers, led by a priest, sang hymns, carried crosses, and looked "more like a religious procession than a workers' demonstration," according to historian Orlando Figes. Nicholas II believed the workers were preparing to attack him. He ordered his soldiers to fire on the parade before he fled the palace. Hundreds were killed or wounded, igniting nationwide strikes and riots. In October 1905, Nicholas promised to grant people "the freedom of conscience, speech, assembly, and association." His October Manifesto, as it was called, also established an elected Duma (legislature). But the czar soon ignored his pledges and in 1906 dissolved the Duma. He carried on with his absolute power still intact.

A military officer, Major-General Konstantin Ivanovich Globachev, later justified the killings on the "second Bloody Sunday." Writing to the Ministry of Internal Affairs, he reported that "the rioting crowds" tried to inflame the troops:

The crowds threw stones and lumps of snow from the street. When the troops fired over the heads of the crowds as a warning . . . they responded with laughter. Only when live rounds were fired into their midst was it possible to disperse the mobs.

Meantime, imperial officials tried to keep news of the uprising from spreading to other cities, but word of the Sunday massacre soon reached citizens in Moscow, southeast of Petrograd.

On that same Sunday, Muscovites (citizens of Moscow) also gathered in the streets. Crowds of students joined in demonstrations. One of the students, Eduard Dune, recalled that news of the Petrograd rebellion swept through Moscow, creating "an extraordinary atmosphere." Like the people in Petrograd, Muscovites believed that a revolution had begun. Dune described the street scene:

> People began to embrace and kiss; strangers became close friends; some wept for joy. In five to ten minutes people seemed reborn. . . .
>
> The crowd grew bigger and bigger, and somewhere in the distance one could hear the well-known refrain of a revolutionary song. By this time it was so crowded that it was impossible to get to one side or the other . . . the street was blocked solid. For the first time in my life I sensed the atmosphere of joy, when everyone you meet seems close to you, your flesh and blood.

SOLDIERS JOIN THE WORKERS

A day after the massacre, February 27, 1917, tens of thousands of soldiers joined rebellious workers in demonstrations. They had become enraged when they learned that some troops had shot innocent people. Rebel soldiers broke into arsenals and stole weapons. They looted homes, businesses, and restaurants. They stormed jails and released prisoners and killed some military and police officers. At the headquarters of the Okhrana, the secret police, they destroyed files that held descriptions of labor organizers—the main targets of the Okhrana. There was no doubt that a full-blown revolution was under way.

Members of the Duma—which was in session at the Tauride Palace in Petrograd—continued to telegraph urgent messages to the czar. They pleaded with the czar to send soldiers from the war front to Petrograd to restore order. Nicholas did not trust the Duma. He believed that some members were exaggerating the importance of the mutiny in an attempt to exert their authority over the government. He ordered the Duma to dissolve. They refused and created the Provisional Committee, a temporary governing body. The committee would try to determine what to do about the protests and the czar.

Some Duma members and military commanders believed that the troop rebellion could spread to the soldiers fighting at the front. They also feared that strikes could disrupt the movement of war supplies to battlefields. On February 27, military commanders were finally able to convince Nicholas that the situation in the capital was grave. The czar ordered a division of loyal imperial troops to travel to Petrograd.

The soldiers first went to the city of Pushkin, south of Petrograd, where the imperial palace Tsarskoe Selo was located. They found that palace guards had joined the mutiny. In Petrograd, the military officers were helpless—half of the 160,000 troops in the city had mutinied. The rest tried to stay out of the conflict, although a few thousand remained loyal to the czar.

THE CZAR ABDICATES

The czar started for Petrograd on February 28, but his train was held up because rebel troops had taken over the rail lines. By then, however, it was already too late for him or his soldiers to make a difference. The Duma declared that the czar should abdicate (step down). They said it was the only way to restore order and assure that Russia would be able to continue to fight in the war.

After hearing opinions from military commanders, Nicholas agreed to abdicate for the good of Russia. He declared that he would turn over the empire to his thirteen-year-old son, Alexis, with the czar's brother Michael as regent. A regent governs until the heir reaches maturity and can rule alone.

Before publicly announcing his abdication, Nicholas consulted a court doctor about his son's health. Alexis was born with hemophilia, a blood-clotting disease. The czar believed that his son soon would be cured. Grigori Rasputin, a self-styled healer who had frequently

Rasputin

WHILE CZAR NICHOLAS II was at the front during World War I, Czarina Alexandra represented him in Petrograd. She sought advice from Grigori Rasputin, a semi-literate peasant, who was known as a holy man and a healer. Rasputin was invited to the court because of his reputation as a healer. The czarina and czar's only son, Alexis, suffered from hemophilia, a bleeding disorder in which the blood does not clot normally. After an injury, a hemophiliac may bleed for a long time, which can be painful and life-threatening. At one time, Rasputin did seem able to stop the uncontrolled bleeding of Alexis, although no one could explain how. This convinced Czarina Alexandra that Rasputin should be available for her son.

Rasputin became court adviser, helping to appoint various officials, many of whom were corrupt and incompetent. As conditions in the country became chaotic, people blamed Rasputin and accused him of having a romantic affair with Alexandra. Members of the Russian nobility murdered Rasputin in December 1916 and dumped his body into a river.

advised the czarina, had predicted that Alexis would be healed in his thirteenth year. The doctor disputed the claim, saying that no medical cure was available.

Nicholas, concerned about his frail son, quickly changed his mind. He declared that he would abdicate in the name of Alexis as well as himself and appoint his brother Michael as successor. Michael, who had not been consulted, refused to become emperor. As a result, the monarchy ceased to exist on March 2, 1917, and the Provisional Committee became the Provisional Government of Russia. The government placed the czar, his wife, son, and four daughters plus servants under arrest at the Alexander Palace near Tsarskoe Selo. Months later they were moved to Ekaterinburg, east of the Ural Mountains. The family was kept under guard in a private home.

"DUAL POWER"

The new Provisional Government was not an elected body. It consisted of government leaders, Duma members, and others who were associated with the bourgeoisie—middle-class merchants and owners of small businesses. Army commanders and various public organizations supported the Provisional Government, and most of the czarist officials remained in their jobs. But there was no longer a legislature.

The Provisional Government promised to create a constituent assembly with members elected by the people. The assembly would prepare a constitution for Russia. But the election was postponed due to wrangling among Russia's diverse political groups. They could not agree on how to proceed and create a fair election process.

As the Provisional Government wrangled, a rival group claimed the right to govern—the Petrograd Soviet of Workers' and Soldiers'

Deputies, or simply Petrograd Soviet. This was a council that had been established in the early 1900s and operated like a local government. Although the Duma had disbanded it earlier, it was reestablished in 1917. Similar worker soviets were set up in fifty different towns. Workers' militias protected the soviets. These paramilitary units—volunteer citizens organized in military fashion—were known as Red Guards.

By the end of March 1917, the Petrograd Soviet had become part of a national network of soviets named the All-Russian Soviet of Workers' and Soldiers' Deputies. Members of these soviets were elected by the proletariat (working class) and soldiers, primarily peasants who had been drafted into the army.

The soviets issued orders to workers, ran factories and railroads, and took charge of post offices and telegraph systems. The Petrograd Soviet shared authority with the Provisional Government. This meant that if, for example, the Provisional Government wanted the streets cleared of protesters, it would need to consult with or get permission from the local soviet. Working-class members of the soviet could easily challenge whatever authority the Provisional Government tried to apply.

POLITICAL PARTIES

About fifty political groups vied for power in Russia in 1917. The major organizations included the Socialist Revolutionary Party (SR), the Bolsheviks, and the Mensheviks. The SRs wanted to seize all land and distribute it among the peasants according to need. They supported a democratically elected constituent assembly. They also advocated a maximum eight-hour day for factory workers.

The Bolsheviks and Mensheviks had earlier belonged to the single Social Democratic Labor Party. They had split in two over differences in how a revolution should be accomplished. The Mensheviks were willing to offer some support for the Provisional Government and wanted a gradual development of socialism, a system in which the government controls industry and agriculture and provides for all its citizens. The Bolsheviks were more radical and wanted immediate revolution. The Bolsheviks were named for the Russian word *bolshinstvo* meaning "majority," while the Mensheviks' name stemmed from *menshinstvo* meaning "minority."

The "dual power" of the Provisional Government and the soviets was essential for the revolution, according to Vladimir Ilyich Lenin, a major revolutionary and political leader. Lenin had founded the Bolshevik Party. The party was based on the teachings of Karl Marx, a nineteenth-century German philosopher. Marx and fellow philosopher Friedrich Engels had written *The Communist Manifesto*. In it Marx and Engels argued that social classes struggle because of economics. People who control the land and means of production (such as factories) accumulate wealth and power, while the proletariat is powerless. They predicted that the proletariat would rise up against the ruling class in a revolution that

Vladimir Ilyich Lenin

would bring about a classless society in an economic system known as communism.

In an April 1917 article published in the Bolshevik newspaper *Pravda*, Lenin explained that dual power "is a revolutionary dictatorship . . . a power directly based on revolutionary seizure, on the direct initiative of the people . . . , and not on a law enacted by a centralized state power."

Later that month, Lenin published another article in *Pravda*, a document that became known as his April Theses. It called for the immediate end to Russia's involvement in the war and for power to be "put into the hands of the proletariat and the poorest section of the peasants." He declared there should be "no support for the Provisional Government" and that "the Soviets of Workers Deputies are the *only possible* form of revolutionary government." Lenin proposed that the police and army should be abolished and that a people's militia should be formed instead. His other proposals included seizing property from landlords, combining all banks to form a national bank, and placing production and the distribution of products under the immediate control of the soviets.

CONFLICTS OVER POWER

With two rival governments, conflicts were bound to occur. One major issue was the war. Members of the Provisional Government supported Russia's war against Germany. So did much of the Russian population. They rejected antiwar messages from the Bolsheviks, who called for immediate peace.

Other issues demanded attention as well. In the countryside, peasants were becoming increasingly militant. They believed they had the right to the land they tilled. The serfs—peasants who by law had been tied to the lands (not allowed to move off it) and required to work for the landowner—had been liberated in 1861. But landowners had kept ownership of most large estates and hired the peasants to work for them as before.

Reports that the czar had abdicated finally reached the country-side in spring 1917. (News traveled slowly during the harsh winter weather.) As the reports circulated, some peasants demanded redistribution of land owned by estate holders. The Provisional Government could do little about land reform—it did not have the money or authority to make changes. The government hoped the constituent assembly, when it convened, would be able to solve the problem. While most farmers were willing to wait for land reform laws, some groups of peasants were impatient and began to seize land for themselves. Orlando Figes, an expert on Russian history, described the scene in one village:

At a preselected time the church bells rang and the peasants assembled with their carts in the middle of the village. Then they moved off towards the manor, like a peasant army, armed with guns, pitchforks, axes, scythes and spades. The squire and his stewards, if they had not already fled, were arrested.

When soldiers (some of them army deserters) returned to their peasant villages, they took part in attacks on the landlords, murdering, burning, and looting. For the most part, though, the peasants' revolutionary actions were tempered by local peasant assemblies. They functioned like local governments, similar to urban soviets. The peasant assemblies passed their own laws regarding land seizures. The regulations prevented extreme violence by allowing peasants to take land in a lawful manner.

"ALL POWER TO THE SOVIETS!"

During the summer months of 1917, Lenin continued to write and publish articles criticizing the Provisional Government. By this time, many in the public had turned against the war. Russia had been losing battles and territory. Citizens were still hungry, and there was still no land reform. Lenin took advantage of the antiwar sentiments to help build support for the Bolshevik Party. He used slogans such as "Peace, Land, and Bread!" and "All Power to the Soviets!"

"The Russian workers bought our country's freedom at the price of their blood. The workers' demands were: bread, freedom, peace.*"*
—V. I. Lenin, 1917

By September 1917, Bolsheviks had won control of the Petrograd Soviet. They established their headquarters at Smolny Institute, a former school for upper-class girls. During early October, Lenin's close associate Leon Trotsky devised tactics for a Bolshevik coup d'état, or armed takeover of the government. Trotsky consulted with other comrades, including Joseph Stalin. These leaders set up a Military Revolutionary Committee (MRC) that acted as a front for the

Bolsheviks. The committee organized the revolt while the Bolsheviks stayed behind the scenes. Unlike the February Revolution, this would not be a broad-based spontaneous uprising. It would be a carefully planned seizure of power by a political group.

The plot was to take control when the All-Russian Congress of Soviets met in Petrograd on October 25, 1917. The Bolshevik representatives, who were in the majority at the congress, approved the takeover. That night, armed Bolsheviks, including Red Guards, seized the Winter Palace and other government buildings, railways, telephone and telegraph systems, and electrical plants. In the morning, October 26, soviets arrested members of the Provisional Government. The Congress of Soviets became the ruling force.

THIS PHOTOGRAPH SHOWS REVOLUTIONARY SOLDIERS SITTING IN THE TAURIDE PALACE, FORMER HOME OF THE RUSSIAN DUMA, AFTER SEIZING THE PALACE IN 1917.

Delegates to the congress chose Lenin to be president of a cabinet known as the Soviet of People's Commissars, or ministers. It was made up entirely of Bolsheviks. Trotsky was named People's Commissar of Foreign Affairs, and Stalin was appointed Commissar of Nationalities. It was Stalin's job to deal with the more than one hundred ethnic groups within the borders of the vast Russian Empire.

Jewish Pogroms

IN RUSSIA DURING THE end of the 1800s, the czar forced most of the empire's 5.5 million Jews to live within fifteen provinces called the Pale of Settlement. Jews could not own land or become officers in the army. Only a limited number of Jewish students were admitted to high schools and universities.

When Czar Alexander II (Nicholas's grandfather) was assassinated in 1881, Jews were accused of the murder and became victims of numerous pogroms, a Russian term meaning "to demolish violently."

Mary Antin in her 1912 book *The Promised Land* noted that, in Russia, the Jewish holiday of Passover was

a time of horror for the Jews. Somebody would start up that lie about murdering Christian children, and the stupid peasants would get mad about it, and fill themselves with vodka, and set out to kill the Jews. They attacked them with knives and clubs and scythes and axes, killed them or tortured them, and burned their houses . . . we lived in fear till the end of the day, knowing that the least disturbance might start a riot, and a riot lead to a pogrom.

Mary Antin's family, like many others subjected to pogroms, left Russia and settled in the United States.

"The chief significance of the October Revolution consists in the fact that the economic betterment of every worker automatically raises the material well-being and culture of the working class as a whole."

—Leon Trotsky, 1923

With the Bolsheviks in control in Petrograd, leaders had to determine how they would govern. More than a dozen political groups opposed the Bolsheviks and were already planning to overthrow them.

In many cities, towns, and villages, people resisted the Bolshevik takeover. For example, in Moscow, teenage cadets (students) from military schools tried to defend the city's Kremlin, or government buildings, and its communication systems. The local Red Guards forced the cadets to surrender, after ten days of fierce street fighting. Moscow's Bolshevik Party then took control of the Moscow government on November 2, 1917.

Bolshevik opponents also included those who wanted the czar returned to power and anarchists who fought against any form of government. Additionally, nationalist groups were against the Bolsheviks. The nationalists included people in Ukraine, Poland, and Finland, then part of the Russian Empire. The Bolsheviks had promised some of these territories autonomy, or the right to self-rule. Each national group wanted to establish a republic—a form of government that gives citizens the right to elect their own leaders. The Bolsheviks had major tasks ahead of them if they were to remain in power.

CHAPTER 2

After the Bolshevik Takeover

A LTHOUGH THE BOLSHEVIKS took power in Petrograd in October 1917, they had to struggle to establish their authority across Russia. The Bolshevik Party was a small political group whose goal was to lead the way to an international revolution against capitalism (private ownership of business and an economy with limited government controls) and launch socialism worldwide. It was not a governmental body. But by the time of the coup, the Bolsheviks controlled the soviets in most major Russian cities and towns. The soviets declared themselves the authority wherever they were established, and soon began terror campaigns to enforce their rule. As Lenin put it: "How can we accomplish a revolution without shooting? Do you think you can settle with your enemies if you disarm? What repressive measures have you then? Imprisonment? Who pays any attention to that in a time of bourgeois war when every party hopes for victory?"

Expanding Power and Issuing Decrees

As national leader of the Bolsheviks, Lenin knew that the party could not concentrate on expanding its power until there was an end to Russia's expenditures of money and personnel in the war against Germany and the other Central Powers. In November 1917, without the consent of the other Allies, he offered an armistice (a cease-fire) to the Germans. He sent Russian representatives to the German military headquarters at Brest-Litovsk, in eastern Poland. After both sides signed the armistice, the fighting between the two countries stopped. Negotiations then began for a Russian peace treaty with Germany.

Meanwhile Lenin had to handle other issues. He knew Russians expected to take part in a national election for the constituent assembly. When elections were held in November 1917, the Bolshevik Party won only one-fourth of the votes. The majority of the votes went to the Social Revolutionaries and Mensheviks. But Lenin did not plan to share power with SRs and Mensheviks. He thought these groups were too moderate and would cooperate with the middle class. The assembly was in session for only two days when Lenin ordered the Red Guards to shut it down forcefully.

More Decrees

Lenin issued more decrees, or orders. One decree issued January 4, 1918, was called the Declaration of Rights of the Working and Exploited People. It banned private ownership of land and declared that all agricultural land and buildings were the "property of the entire working people." Workers gained control of factories and were granted an eight-hour workday. Previously most workers labored twelve to fourteen hours each day. The declaration also required everyone of all classes to work. Another order called for "the complete disarming of the propertied classes."

The Decree on the Separation of Church and State, on January 20, 1918, declared that all church property belonged to the nation—not only land but also church statues and artwork. The Russian Orthodox Christian Church had always endorsed the czar as appointed by God. It was conservative, worked closely with the czar's government, and didn't look kindly on change. Marx's socialism was atheistic—it opposed all religion—so even religious education was forbidden. With these decrees, the Bolshevik Red Guards justified a war of terror on the middle class, landowners, and the church.

The Liberation of Serfs

DURING THE 1800S, ABOUT half of the forty million Russian peasants were serfs. That is, they were almost slaves, unable to move from the property they lived on, which was owned by the nobility, the czar, and religious organizations. In the mid-1800s, Czar Alexander II realized that his empire needed reforms and that Russia's economy based on the labor of serfs could not match that of industrialized nations. In February 1861, he issued an Emancipation Manifesto that accompanied legislation to grant serfs their freedom and land. That left landowners without a large labor force, so the legislation included a provision that the serfs had to pay the landowner for their land. The government would advance the total amount for the land to the landowner; the peasants were required to repay the money to the government over a period of forty-nine years. Few peasants could afford this plan, and payments were eventually cancelled in 1907.

Terror

The Bolshevik leaders began to speak out against the bourgeoisie and the wealthy classes, blaming them for trying to undermine the revolution. Lenin charged:

> The bourgeoisie are prepared to commit the most heinous crimes; they are bribing the outcast and degraded elements of society and plying them with drink to use them in riots. The supporters of the bourgeoisie, particularly among the higher clerical staff, bank officials, and so on, are sabotaging their work, and are organising strikes to thwart the government's measures for the realisation of socialist reforms. They have even gone so far as to sabotage food distribution, thereby menacing millions of people with famine. . . . Urgent measures are necessary to fight the counter-revolutionaries and saboteurs.

Some of those "urgent measures" included sending Red Army units to villages and towns to threaten and terrorize residents who were seen as enemies of the revolution. Zinaida Zhemchuzhnaia, a high school teacher, witnessed the behavior of Red Army soldiers in the Kuban region of southern Russia:

> They were dusty, dirty, and shabby, and had cartridge belts draped across their chests, rifles slung over their shoulders, and revolvers resting on their hips. . . . Most of them were drunk because the first thing they always did was to loot the wine cellars.

At five o'clock a rally was convened in front of the town hall. The commissar [military officer], who was completely drunk, caught sight of the priest in the crowd. He told him to come closer and then, without saying a word, pulled out his revolver and killed him right on the spot. The crowd gasped. The kindly old priest was beloved by the townspeople. . . . With one shot the commissar had quenched the flickering hope that the [new] government was a true and just power. . . . After the brutal murder of the priest there were no more illusions. The Bolsheviks had shown their true face.

In many cities, towns, and villages the Red soldiers broke into homes and churches to take food, money, silverware, furniture, jewelry, furs, wine, or anything else they wanted. Families were driven from their homes. Frequently, they forced several homeless families to move in with people who had been able to keep their homes.

Eugenia Peacock and her family, who had come from England to live in Russia, were evicted from an estate owned by her Russian grandmother's family. It was near the town of Torzhok in Tver province, northwest of Moscow. Eugenia was about six years old when soldiers arrived to take over the estate. Many years later, Peacock recalled:

They gave us three days to pack up what we could take with us and they camped out in front of the house in tents. They allowed each family to take one peasant cart and horse to carry themselves and their belongings as far as Torzhok. The carts and horses were then to be sent back. . . . There was no question of taking any furniture . . . just some clothes and personal things. My parents packed what they could, and my mother, father, grandmother, myself and the driver, who had to take the horse and cart back, went to Torzhok.

For many working-class Russians, "disarming the propertied classes" meant changing places with the rich. As one former servant put it, "I've spent all my life in the stables while they [the rich] . . . lie on soft couches playing with their poodles. No more of that, I say! It's my turn to play with poodles now; and, as for them, it is their turn to go and work in the stables." The new government forced wealthy people to clean streets, dig ditches, and do other types of physical labor. Such work was meant to humble the rich, to make them struggle like peasants, servants, and factory workers.

RED ARMY SOLDIERS GUARD A GROUP OF WEALTHY RUSSIANS WHO HAVE BEEN TAKEN HOSTAGE DURING THE RUSSIAN REVOLUTION. THE RICH WERE SEEN AS THE ENEMY OF THE WORKING CLASS.

On February 1, 1918, Lenin issued another order. It changed the calendar. From that day forward, Lenin declared, Russians would follow the Western Gregorian (New Style) calendar, which was thirteen days ahead of the Old Style calendar. Immediately, February 1 became February 14, 1918.

When the Bolshevik Party held a congress in March 1918, Lenin declared that the party should change its name to the Communist Party. In his view, the change would show that the Bolsheviks planned to realize the goal of communism, as outlined by Marx and Engels in *The Communist Manifesto*.

Negotiations and Preparations for Peace

The Allies hoped that Russia's negotiations for a separate peace treaty with Germany would fall apart and Russians would rejoin the fighting. But Russian soldiers were exhausted and no match for Germany's much stronger army. Russian troops had been retreating and deserting in large numbers. More than one million deserted in 1918.

As negotiations went on into February 1918, German officials became impatient. They threatened to take over Russian cities if a peace treaty was not signed. Lenin feared that the Central Powers could invade and occupy much of his country. So on February 21, he issued a decree called "The Socialist Fatherland in Danger!"

Printed in newspapers the next day, the decree declared that Russia's "entire manpower and resources" would be used to defend the revolution. It ordered railroad companies to "do their utmost to prevent the enemy" from taking over the transportation system. "All grain and food stocks generally, as well as all valuable property in danger of falling into the enemy's hands, must be unconditionally destroyed." A further order required all "able-bodied members of the bourgeois class" to dig trenches "under the supervision of Red Guards; those who resist are to be shot." The government took control of newspapers and books and censored free speech. Finally, the decree declared that any enemy agents, agitators, spies, or enemies of the revolution must "be shot on the spot."

The decree did not explain what evidence would determine who were enemy agents, agitators, or spies, or whether suspects had committed any crimes. Anyone suspected of being a counterrevolutionary, or against the Bolsheviks, could be executed without a trial or proof of guilt. To find and eliminate Bolshevik enemies, Lenin founded a secret police unit called the All-Russian Extraordinary Commission for Struggle against Counter-Revolution and Sabotage, known by its Russian initials as Cheka.

Effects of Brest-Litovsk Treaty

Russia signed the Brest-Litovsk Treaty with the Central Powers on March 3, 1918. As part of the treatry, Russia gave up a large portion of the western part of the empire—32 percent of its productive farmland, plus factories, railway systems, coal and iron mines, and other resources.

Under terms of the treaty, Russia lost 62 million citizens. Germany and Austria-Hungary took over formerly Russian-controlled Poland and the Baltic states of Lithuania, Latvia, and Estonia. Russia ceded parts of the southern Caucasus, between the Black Sea and the Caspian Sea, to Turkey. The former Russian territories of Ukraine, Georgia, and Finland gained independence. As part of the agreement, Germany declared it would order soldiers into Ukraine to help support its independence.

For the majority of Russians, the treaty was shameful. Even those who had called for peace condemned their country's losses and turned against Lenin and the Bolsheviks. Some believed the Bolsheviks had betrayed the revolution by surrendering to Germany. There was so much resentment that Lenin feared people who had supported the former czar would try to restore the imperial government.

Even though Nicholas II and his family were under house arrest, Lenin worried that supporters might try to rescue them. He ordered the Cheka to execute Nicholas. Cheka agents decided to execute the entire family, their physician, and servants. In July 1918, all were assassinated in the basement of the house where they were imprisoned. Their bodies were burned and the remains buried.

Anarchists vs. Bolsheviks

Many anarchists, who had joined with the Bolsheviks in 1917 to help topple the czarist regime, were outraged when they learned about the peace treaty. They openly criticized Bolshevik rule, even though this meant their lives were in danger. In Moscow and Petrograd, the anarchists formed units of Black Guards, named for the anarchists' black flag. They armed themselves with guns and grenades as protection against possible Bolshevik attacks.

The Cheka raided anarchist centers in Moscow and Petrograd, killing or wounding forty. Hundreds of anarchists were arrested and imprisoned. To prevent further criticism of Bolshevik rule, the Cheka shut down anarchist newspapers and journals. Some anarchists went underground—kept their activities secret. Others went to Ukraine, where peasants had formed anarchist communes. These were groups whose members shared what they produced.

Peter Arshinov, a leading anarchist, had organized Russian workers during the czarist regime and was often jailed for his activities. While serving a sentence in a Moscow prison from 1911 to 1917, he had become friends with another anarchist, Nestor Makhno, from Ukraine. After the two were released from prison in March 1917, Arshinov worked with anarchists in Moscow. Makhno returned to Gulyai-Polye to organize peasants.

Makhno and His Guerrillas

In his home village, Makhno began to put into practice his view of anarchism. He declared:

Anarchism's outward form is a free, non-governed society, which offers freedom, equality and solidarity for its members. Its foundations are to be found in man's sense of mutual responsibility, which has remained unchanged in all places and times. This sense of responsibility is capable of securing freedom and social justice for all men by its own unaided efforts. It is also the foundation of true communism.

To fight for "freedom and social justice," he organized a guerrilla army called the Revolutionary Insurgent Army of the Ukraine, known as the Makhnovists. His purpose was to wage war against those who tried to destroy Ukraine's independence and the true revolution which was led by anarchists. Makhno claimed that the Makhnovists, not the Bolsheviks, supported workers and peasants. In his words, "the land belongs to nobody and it can be used only by those who care about it and cultivate it." His guerrillas carried a black flag with the slogan

"The Land to the Peasants, the Factories to the Workers."

Peasants and workers in Ukraine were especially hostile to the Bolshevik government, following the agreement with the Central Powers. At least five hundred thousand German and Austrian troops occupied Ukraine, though they actually had little interest in defending Ukrainian independence. Troops forcefully took grain, poultry, eggs, livestock, and other goods. According to Arshinov, "Hundreds, even thousands of trains, carried everything off. When the peasants resisted this pillage and tried to retain the fruits of their labor," they were beaten and shot.

The Makhnovists attacked not only the German and Austrian occupation forces but also Ukrainian landowners and government authorities. The guerrillas would appear suddenly, and, as Arshinov described it:

[T]hey fell thunderously on some estates, massacred all the sworn enemies of the peasants, and disappeared as rapidly as they had come. The next day Makhno would be more than a hundred miles away, would appear in some town, massacre the *Varta* [security police], officers and noblemen, and vanish before the German troops had time to realize what had happened.

Wherever Makhno and his army liberated a town or village from German occupation, peasants and workers were able to take charge of their lives and work as they saw fit. Political prisoners were released from jails, and people were able to write and speak freely.

The Germans finally left Ukraine when World War I ended on November 11, 1918. Two days later, the Bolsheviks cancelled the Treaty of Brest-Litovsk and regained the lands that had been given to Germany. But ending the treaty did not increase their popularity. The Bolsheviks' numerous enemies were ready to do battle against them.

CHAPTER 3

Civil War

A T LEAST A DOZEN GROUPS in diverse parts of Russia took up arms in 1918 against Lenin and his Communist Party. In a civil war that lasted until the end of 1920, these groups battled on numerous fronts, primarily in eastern, southern, and northwestern Russia. In general, the various groups sided with either the anti-Communists, who were called Whites, or with the Communists, who were known as Reds.

The Whites included nobles, former military officials, and middle-class property owners. They organized three main military forces, but each group operated independently under separate commanders. The Whites hoped to restore the Provisional Government and the Constituent Assembly. A few Whites wanted to restore the czar.

The Reds, named for the color long associated with revolutionaries, were primarily urban workers. Their Red Army consisted of factory workers and volunteers from the Petrograd and Moscow Red Guards. They were led by Trotsky, Commissar of War. He was intent on saving the revolution. To achieve that goal, the Red Army sought and for short periods gained the support of Makhno and his Ukrainian

> *"No matter what one thinks of Bolshevism, it is undeniable that the Russian Revolution is one of the great events of human history, and the rise of the Bolsheviki [members of the Bolshevik Party] a phenomenon of world-wide importance."*
>
> —John Reed, American journalist,
> *Ten Days That Shook the World*, 1919

anarchists. But such an alliance was only a matter of convenience. Lenin hoped to capture Makhno and bring the anarchists under the control of the Communists. On his part, Makhno and rebel peasants and workers wanted no part of soviets that were controlled by the Communists. Their fight was for freedom from all state authority and liberty for the masses of workers and peasants.

THE CZECH LEGION AGAINST THE REDS

The Communists also faced another enemy: Czechoslovakian soldiers. Czechoslovakia (the modern Czech Republic and Slovakia) was controlled by Austria-Hungary, and Czech men had been forced to join Austro-Hungarian armies during World War I. Up to sixty thousand Czech soldiers had been captured by Russians. The czar's government had released some of these prisoners of war and created the Czech

Legion, a military body of thirty thousand to thirty-five thousand troops. The Czech soldiers agreed to fight with Russia against Germany and the other Central Powers.

After the Brest-Litovsk Treaty, the Czechs feared that they would be recaptured by Austrians or Germans. Lenin gave them permission to join French forces fighting Germany in Europe. They hoped that France and the other Allies would help establish an independent Czechoslovakian nation at the end of the war.

In the spring of 1918, the Czech Legion began its trip to western Europe. The soldiers were allowed to take a few weapons for self-defense. They could not travel the shortest route over Russia's western border because it passed through German-held territory. So instead, the Czechs went east. They began their journey on the Trans-Siberian Railway.

The railway begins in Moscow, crosses southern Russia and southern Siberia to the eastern port city of Vladivostok on the Sea of Japan. The journey covers more than 6,000 miles (9,000 km). At Vladivostock the Czechs planned to travel by ship to the United States, cross that country to its east coast, and board a ship to Europe. It was literally to be a trip around the world.

The Czech Legion traveled peacefully at first. But local soviets along the route were wary of foreign soldiers who stopped at their railway stations. At some places, Red Guard units tried to disarm the

FAST FACT

CONSTRUCTION OF RUSSIA'S TRANS-SIBERIAN RAILROAD BEGAN IN 1891 UNDER CZAR ALEXANDER III. IN MODERN TIMES, IT IS THE LONGEST UNBROKEN RAIL LINE IN THE WORLD. THE ROUTE FROM MOSCOW TO VLADIVOSTOK IS 6,152 MILES (9,288 KM).

Czechs. They were not successful. The Czechs began to suspect that the Reds were trying to capture them and turn them over to Germany. They grew more distrustful when they discovered in April that Trotsky had ordered half of the Czech troops to turn around and leave Russia by way of Arkhangelsk, a seaport in northwestern Russia. But the Czechs had no intention of going back. They decided to fight their way across southern Russia and Siberia to Vladivostok.

In mid-May, they fought with Red Guards in the city of Cheliabinsk in west-central Russia. The Czechs won the skirmish and took the Red Guards' weapons. When Trotsky learned of the incident he ordered the soviets along the railway to shoot any Czech soldier found carrying a weapon.

CZECH SOLDIERS USE BRANCHES TO CAMOUFLAGE THEIR TRAIN AS IT TRAVELS THROUGH RUSSIA IN 1918. THE SOLDIERS ARE AT THE READY IN CASE OF ATTACK.

To the Czechs, Trotsky's order meant that the Communists had betrayed them. Until the end of June, the Czechs fought Red Guards and captured at least eight towns along the way to Vladivostok. They were helped by Socialist Revolutionaries and Mensheviks who had fled to Siberia to escape the Communists after the October coup.

When World War I ended in November 1918, the Allies began efforts to send rescue ships to Vladivostok. Dozens of ships arrived in April 1919, and by the end of May, nearly all of the Czechs were evacuated. The last of the Czech Legion left Russia in August 1919.

The Greens

During some Civil War skirmishes, both Reds and Whites had to contend with bands of peasants known as Greens. Their name came from the woodlands where they lived, primarily in valleys along the Volga River. They identified themselves with green branches and leaves in their hats.

Most Greens were peasants who had been drafted into either Red or White armies and had deserted. They found refuge in the wooded areas and strongly defended any attempts to invade their territory. The Greens were especially bitter that both the Reds and Whites seized grain from peasant villages. Peasants were left with little or nothing, and starvation was common. The Greens often attacked and killed those who came for their food supplies.

Sometimes, Cossacks joined the Greens. Cossacks were independent groups and were not loyal to any political party. Their military skills and horsemanship were well known throughout Russia, and many Cossacks had served in the czar's cavalry. They did not care who was in power as long as they could maintain their independence.

The Cossacks

COSSACKS ARE A COMMUNITY of people who have lived for years in the southern regions of Russia, Ukraine, Siberia, and northern Kazakhstan. Known for their military skills, especially on horseback, Cossack units were used to put down uprisings during czarist times. They fought for both the Red Army and the White Army during the Russian Civil War. In Ukraine, Cossacks are considered national heroes because for hundreds of years they defended their land from foreign invaders.

The Cossacks lived on communal lands in western and southern Russia. They had been given land by nineteenth-century czars in exchange for protecting Russia's borders. Cossack territory on the Don River in southern Russia had declared its independence from Russia in November 1917.

By the time the Civil War started, Rostov-on-Don, a major city in Cossack territory, had become a haven for the former czar's military officers, businesspeople, and some counterrevolutionary politicians. These Whites believed that the Cossacks would support a return to imperial rule.

The Whites built a force called the Volunteer Army in Rostov. They convinced the Cossacks to fight with them against the Red Army. The Whites argued that this was the only way to defend Cossack independence, since non-Cossacks in the region sided with the Reds.

RED ARMY DEFEATS

During 1918 the Red Army suffered numerous defeats, partly because peasants who had been drafted frequently deserted. In 1918 more than one million men were Red Army runaways. Three years later, deserters totaled nearly four million. The army could not bring in enough peasant draftees to replace the escapees.

The Red Army also was hampered by the need to fight on many different fronts. As Russian student Eduard M. Dune, who became a Red Guard and joined the Red Army, explained: Red Army "regiments were stationed in the region around Astrakhan" in southeastern Russia. Others were fighting the White's Volunteer Army along the Kuban River and near the Black Sea, while "28 regiments were sent to the Ukraine . . . 38 regiments formed on the German and

Cavalry "Boy"

ZINAIDA PATRIKEEVA, A YOUNG factory worker, was the only woman in one Red Army cavalry unit that fought the Whites during the Civil War of 1918 to 1920. Many years later, she recalled that she created a uniform of sorts: "I cut my wide skirt up the middle, sewed on some buttons, and made something resembling pants. I was also given a greatcoat, a tall sheepskin hat, and boots. After that I looked like a cavalry boy." She was involved in a fight at Rostov-on-Don, a city where the Whites had built a strong military force. Her cavalry unit clashed with a White regiment and engaged in hand-to-hand combat. As she described it:

Revolver in hand, I cut through a crowd of officers and fired all seven bullets, killing several people. . . . At Rostov we captured many rifles and artillery pieces. It was a glorious victory! . . .

I was given a Maxim machine gun. I attached it to my saddle and always carried it with me. As soon as the fighting began, I would dismount and shower those White bastards with bullets.

Finnish fronts." Sixty-five regiments were on a front along the border with Poland and Latvia, while "97 regiments were sent to the eastern front . . . and 44 regiments went to the Don to fight the Cossacks." In brief, Dune wrote, "enemies appeared on all sides."

In 1919 the White Volunteer Army was led by Anton Denikin, who planned to move his forces from a base in Rostov toward Moscow, the new Communist capital. His goal was to capture the capital city and overthrow the Reds. East of the Ural Mountains in Siberia, Alexander Kolchak, former commander-in-chief of Russia's land and naval forces, also was building an army to attack the Reds. So was a White general in the north, Nikolai Yudenich. His troops were threatening Petrograd.

All of the anti-Red troops received help from capitalistic countries that wanted to stop the spread of communism. Some, including the United States, Great Britain, Japan, and France, sent troops to aid the Whites on the northern, eastern, and southern fronts. These allies stationed their ships in various ports. They also provided the White armies with thousands of rifles and machine guns, plus ammunition, tanks, and airplanes. With such aid, many nations, as well as many Russians, thought the Reds would be overthrown easily.

Petrograd in Danger

Victor Serge, a French anarchist and revolutionary journalist, feared that the Communist revolution in Russia was in danger. He was in Petrograd during May and June 1919 and wrote:

> The White army is gathering outside Petrograd. Everywhere it has gone it has left a trail of blood behind it. . . . I don't think

that ever, anywhere, the contempt for life and for human suffering have been systematically developed in such a degraded fashion. . . . Our newspapers are full of such stories. . . . Torture, hanging, shooting, slaughter with cold steel, beatings and sham trials. . . . I know very well that if the Whites enter the city all those who are dear to me can expect no mercy. . . . We can sense the approach of terror just as before thunderstorms you can feel the air charged with electricity.

A few months later, in September, *New York Times* journalist Harold Williams was in Rostov to report on Denikin and the Volunteer Army. Denikin was preparing to move against Moscow. In a cable to the *Times*, Williams noted:

The volunteer army now has broad scope for its operations. . . . Denikin's authority now extends not only over the Cossack region but also over a wide stretch of territory between the Volga and the Dnieper [rivers]. He commands the Black Sea coast between Georgia and Bessarabia, and has under his control such important cities as Kharkov, Kiev and Odessa.

By October 1919, Yudenich's White troops were ready to storm Petrograd. But Trotsky went to the city to organize Red defenses. He armed workers and ordered military forces from Moscow to transfer to Petrograd. Within a few weeks, Petrograd's Red Army outnumbered Yudenich's three to one. Yudenich gave up his attack and withdrew his army. As Serge reported: "This morning, 30 October, a total change in the situation. . . . Petrograd is indeed saved! The Red republic is saved!"

THE RED ARMY SURGES

The threat of attacks on Petrograd and Moscow caused much distress among the Communist leaders. The area between Petrograd and Moscow was Russia's heartland, with a large population and industrial base. In 1919 Lenin sent a letter to the Central Committee of the Russian Communist Party:

> All Communists first and foremost, all sympathisers with them, all honest workers and peasants, all Soviet officials must *pull themselves together like soldiers* and concentrate *to the maximum their work*, their efforts and their concern *directly on the tasks of the war*. . . . The Soviet Republic is besieged by the enemy. It must become a *single military camp*, not in word but in deed. All the work of all institutions most be adapted to the war and placed on a military footing!

Two million Russians were drafted into the Red Army in 1919, bringing the total to three million. (The following year, the force reached five million.) The Reds far outnumbered the Whites, whose armies totaled about two hundred fifty thousand. Military supplies available to the Reds also were superior to those the White army obtained from its allies. The Red Army had taken over the arsenals of the former czar and had access to weapons and munitions factories under Communist control in the heartland of the country. Another Red advantage was its resolute purpose: to unite all the former empire under a Communist government. The Reds never lost sight of that goal.

The White armies were never unified. They did not even have a central command. Their forces were separated by thousands of miles

A GROUP OF NEWLY DRAFTED RED ARMY SOLDIERS PREPARE TO FIGHT IN THE CIVIL WAR. AMONG THE DRAFTEES ARE WOMEN AND ELDERLY MEN.

along the borders of the former empire. They seldom communicated with each other, because the Reds controlled the telegraph and transportation systems.

Wherever the Whites fought, they did little or nothing to encourage political support from the local people. Their leaders were more concerned about military maneuvers than politics, and they paid little attention to the interests of the people they controlled. All these factors, plus Red superiority in workers and armaments, began to change the direction of the Civil War in the Reds' favor during the later months of 1919.

Yudenich's retreat from Petrograd was just the beginning of White withdrawals. Kolchak had to retreat from his Siberian headquarters in Omsk. In the west, Reds took over Kiev and Kharkov, once held by Whites. By the end of the 1919, masses of White soldiers and civilians were trying to escape by European and U.S. ships that were still in port on the Black Sea.

White troops in the Crimea, a peninsula in the Black Sea, held on over the next year, but they too fell to the Reds, in November 1920. As the year ended, so did the Civil War. It had killed an estimated one million to two million Reds and Whites in combat.

"The air is permeated with a vague smell of blood, creating among us a state of mind in which terror cannot fail to grow."
—Victor Serge, writing about the Civil War, 1919

WAR COMMUNISM

While the Civil War was under way, the Communist Party established an economic system known as War Communism. A main provision of the system was the nationalization of land and industries. In other words, the government took over ownership of private property and businesses in areas that it controlled, such as those around Moscow and Petrograd. Workers no longer had the right to operate factories. Instead Communist managers were put in charge. Workers had to abide by strict government rules. Private markets—free exchange of goods and services—were forbidden.

Under War Communism, industries manufactured war materials, not consumer goods. The government also controlled agricultural production. Food production had been declining, due in part to the drafting of many peasant farmers. Other peasants had gone to urban areas to work in factories.

As the war progressed, city residents faced shortages of food, fuel, clothing, and other basic necessities. The government required peasant villages to turn over any surplus grain and produce to feed the cities. Russian peasants traditionally lived in a mir, or commune. Under this arrangement, the village owned the land and peasants farmed it jointly. Officials sent armed men to villages to take by force whatever they determined was surplus—grain, produce, cattle, or horses. They often beat or killed the peasants who resisted. The food patrols assumed that peasants—especially rich peasants, known as kulaks—were hoarding what they produced. Indeed, many peasants did hide their grain, potatoes, or other produce for fear they would not have enough for themselves and their families.

Lenin hated kulaks and repeatedly insisted that they were greedy and "rabid foes of the Soviet government." He accused the kulaks of being leeches that "have sucked the blood of the working people and grown richer as the workers in the cities and factories starved."

Yet the small number of peasants labeled kulaks could hardly have been responsible for widespread food shortages. At the time, there were more than 100 million people in the nation, and 80 percent were peasant farmers. The so-called rich among them made up only 2 percent of all peasants.

In reality, kulaks were peasant families who worked hard on their farms; built their own huts; and made their own furniture, utensils, clothes, and bedding. They lived and survived on their own, always trying to better themselves. Such achievers went against Communist practices. Kulaks became scapegoats—people that Lenin and other Communists could blame—for the failings of War Communism.

By blaming kulaks, Lenin tried to stir up class warfare between rich and poor peasants. He believed that poor peasants would become Red supporters and rise up against their wealthier neighbors. But when food armies came to villages to confiscate supplies, peasants of all kinds banded together to fight back. At least 245 peasant revolts took place in the first year under Communist rule alone, and many other peasant rebellions followed over the next two years.

Urban Food Shortages

The armed food patrols did little to ease the severe shortages in urban areas. City people began to take bags of their personal belongings to the countryside to barter or exchange for food, a practice called bagging. Thirty pounds (13 kilograms) of kerosene (fuel), for example, was worth 1 pound (0.5 kg) of flour. A pair of boots could be exchanged for a pound (0.5 kg) of potatoes.

Food and other goods could also be purchased on the black market (an illegal network of buyers and sellers). But few could afford the high prices. A person might sell a coat and have only enough money to buy a few eggs or some soap.

One woman who experienced the shortages in Moscow was Dorothy Russell. Her father had been a tutor to a duke and a prince. Because he was British, he was arrested by the Reds and imprisoned. The family, including Dorothy, who was a young teenager at the time, had to go to work. Like most city people, they had to search for food. Russell reported years later:

Sometimes we bought bread on the black market; mother got some once and it was so awful that she gave a piece of it to a friend of the family, a doctor, and he discovered that it was 95 percent other matter, including old soldiers' coats and dust from the road, and only 5 percent flour . . . we couldn't even cut it with a chopper.

Apart from bread, we had things fried in cod-liver oil and castor oil. Mother once bought twelve dozen eggs from a salesman, and she picked out five that were good; the rest were rotten, really rotten—they stank to high heaven. . . . Frying things in castor oil isn't very tasty, and we used to have to fry . . . frozen potato ends, and they're slimy and horrible.

To survive, thousands of workers stole fuel, tools, and other items from the factories where they were employed and traveled every day to peasant villages to trade what they stole for food. Other workers made things to trade. Some made shoe soles from conveyor belts, for example,

New Pogroms against the Jews

DURING THE CIVIL WAR, Christians blamed Jews for economic problems and political and social unrest, leading to pogroms that were organized locally, sometimes with government and police encouragement. According to the United States Holocaust Memorial Museum, "During the civil war that followed the 1917 Bolshevik Revolution, Ukrainian nationalists, Polish officials, and Red Army soldiers all engaged in pogrom-like violence in western Belorussia [Belarus] and Poland's Galicia province [West Ukraine], killing tens of thousands of Jews between 1918 and 1920." Up to two thousand pogroms took place in Ukraine alone. There is no exact number known of Jews killed during the Civil War pogroms, but one estimate is that more than 150,000 died.

and others made tools from iron bars. Communists did not approve of this private trade, but they could not stop it. Without the trade, even Lenin had to admit that millions of urban residents would have starved.

As shortages continued, workers who had once lived in the countryside began to leave urban industries and return to their home villages. In October 1917, there were 3.6 million industrial workers. That number dropped to 1.5 million by 1920. Industries had to close because they lacked skilled workers.

Throughout the country, the rail system had shut down or was in disarray. Trains were unable to transport goods. Raw materials, such as coal and iron ore, could not get to factories that were still functioning. Some industries that produced cotton goods could not do so because no raw cotton was available. Most farmland was being used to grow food. Russia's economy was in collapse. Lenin eventually realized that War Communism was a failure. He would have to devise a new economic plan.

CHAPTER 4

A Country in Chaos

MANY RUSSIANS BELIEVED that with the end of the Civil War, the promises made in the aftermath of the 1917 revolution would be kept. People hoped the Communists would help establish life with fewer restrictions and more liberties. Workers hoped for changes in the economic policies of War Communism and the restoration of industries. But to maintain control, the Communists continued their oppression of workers and peasants. They also sent funds to revolutionaries in western Europe, still hoping to create uprisings and a worldwide communist revolution.

CHAOS AFTER THE REVOLUTION

The winter of 1919 to 1920 was a desperate time in Russian cities. Most people were always hungry, and they lacked clothing to stay warm. Since no clothing was being produced, people recycled whatever they could find. They made coats from rugs and hats from felt material torn from pool tables.

Fuel was extremely difficult to find too, and friends and families gathered to get warm wherever they could keep temperatures above freezing. People tore down fences and other wooden structures to use as fuel for their fires.

Emma Goldman, a well-known American anarchist, was appalled by the chaotic and life-threatening conditions in Russia. Goldman was born in Russia but had lived in the United States for three decades. The U.S. government had deported her and other anarchists to Russia because of their antigovernment activities. She and anarchist Alexander Berkman arrived in January 1920. Goldman could not believe what she heard and observed. She was a firm believer in the revolution, but she learned that the aftermath of the revolution was not as she had envisioned it.

Goldman traveled to Russian cities and towns to see firsthand what the revolution had accomplished. She was dismayed at the oppression of workers. To her great disappointment, she found that Russia did not even approach the communist ideal that was supposed to be the basis for the revolution.

Communists were killing hundreds of counterrevolutionaries. Prisons were filled with anti-Communist workers and peasants. Goldman sought the opinion of Maxim Gorky, a well-known Russian writer and spokesperson for the revolution. Gorky reminded her that "revolution is a grim and relentless task." Although Gorky was Lenin's friend and supported the revolution, he publicly criticized Lenin's repression of intellectuals, writers, and artists. Lenin was afraid that these groups would promote freedom of thought and expression and undermine his Communist regime.

Goldman also aired her complaints about Communist abuses to Lenin, but he advised her not to grieve over spilled blood. The blood was justified in Lenin's view, because Russia was paving the way for a world revolution. The Communists had no intention of yielding to proletariat demands, Goldman concluded.

KRONSTADT REBELLION

During the early months of 1921, workers in Petrograd staged a massive strike. They protested their low wages, high food prices, and lack of fuel. They objected to doing without while Bolshevik leaders obtained whatever they needed. Workers also had political demands. They wanted freedom of speech and the press, and the release of workers who had been imprisoned because of their protests. Communist leaders ordered the strikers to go back to work. Workers refused, and strikes erupted in other cities.

Communist leaders tried to prevent news of worker protests from reaching Kronstadt, a naval fortress about 20 miles (32 km) west of Petrograd on an island in the Gulf of Finland. Russia's Baltic Fleet was stationed there. The Kronstadt sailors were known as radicals; they had mutinied during the 1905 uprising against the czar. They also had been part of the 1917 Bolshevik revolution. Many of these sailors were on warships that had been the main defense of the Bolsheviks. Crewmembers had acted as guards for Lenin during his first days in power. But they turned against the Reds when they learned about the worker protests in messages sent by family and friends. The government actions against workers and the continued seizure of food from peasants especially angered the sailors, who were mainly from peasant families.

Sailors and soldiers at Kronstadt had no intention of deserting the revolution. As anarchist Berkman pointed out, the sailors and artillerymen "were the staunchest supporters of the Soviet system, but they were opposed to the dictatorship of any political party."

A naval crew went to Petrograd in late February 1921 to visit factories and learn about the strikes. The delegation found embittered workers who had counted on their voices being heard in the soviets but instead faced a Communist Party with absolute power.

The delegation returned to Kronstadt to report its findings on March 1. A provisional revolutionary committee was established to confront the Communist government and present more than a dozen demands. They included:

- new elections to soviets, because members no longer expressed the wishes of the workers and peasants;
- freedom of speech and the press for workers, peasants, and anarchists;
- release of all political prisoners;
- elimination of political groups in the armed forces;
- granting peasants freedom to farm as they wished on their own soil and to own cattle.

The Communist leaders saw the challenge from Kronstadt as an attack on the revolution. Lenin accused the Kronstadters of being used by Whites plotting to overthrow Reds. He and Trotsky denounced the rebellion and set up a blockade, preventing food and ammunition from reaching Kronstadt over the thick ice that covered the gulf.

In the spring, which was soon approaching, the ice would melt, and the Kronstadt rebels could receive reinforcements and supplies by sea. Trotsky had to act quickly. On March 7, he sent a Red Army force across 5 miles (8 km) of ice in the gulf to attack Kronstadt. Berkman, who was in Petrograd, wrote in his diary that day:

> Distant rumbling reaches my ears. . . . It sounds again, stronger and nearer, as if rolling toward me. All at once I realize that artillery is being fired. It is 6 P.M. Kronstadt has been attacked!
>
> Days of anguish and cannonading [artillery attacks]. My heart is numb with despair; something has died within me.

REBEL FORCES AT KRONSTADT AWAIT THE RED ARMY ABOARD A BATTLESHIP DURING THE MARCH 1921 KRONSTADT REBELLION.

The people on the streets look bowed with grief, bewildered. No one trusts himself to speak. The thunder of heavy guns rends the air.

The Red troops that attacked were young and inexperienced. They tried to retreat, but Kronstadt artillerymen shot them down. On March 17, Trotsky sent an army of fifty thousand to attack Kronstadt. As the Reds began to overpower the naval base, thousands of Kronstadt citizens and sailors fled to Finland. Government forces took control of the base and executed hundreds of sailors. No exact figures are available, but thousands on both sides died in the attack.

Disillusionment

The terrible slaughter and other atrocities of the Reds convinced Berkman and Goldman that the revolution had taken the wrong direction. Berkman wrote in his diary on September 30, 1921:

One by one the embers of hope have died out. . . . Dictatorship is trampling the masses under the foot. The revolution is dead; its spirit cries in the wilderness. The Bolshevik myth must be destroyed. I have decided to leave Russia.

Berkman and Goldman, disheartened, left Russia at the end of 1921. Later Goldman wrote in her autobiography:

In the train, December 1, 1921! My dreams crushed, my faith broken, my heart like a stone[.] *Matushka Rossiya* [Mother Russia] bleeding from a thousand wounds, her soil strewn with the dead. I clutch the bar at the frozen window-pane and grit my teeth to suppress my sobs.

New Economic Policy

The Kronstadt mutiny was for the most part a rebellion against War Communism. Lenin realized that the open rebellion of soldiers and sailors, strikes, and peasant unrest were jeopardizing the goal of achieving Communism. He admitted that War Communism had been a blunder. As Trotsky wrote years later, "The collapse of the productive forces surpassed anything of the kind that history had ever seen. The country, and the government with it, were at the very edge of the abyss."

All production of all kinds had fallen. For example, 80 million tons (72.5 metric tons) of grain had been produced the year before World War I, in 1913, but in 1921 only 37.6 million tons (34 million metric tons) were produced. Coal production fell from 29 million tons (26.3 metric tons) in 1913 to 9 million tons (8 million metric tons) in 1921. During that same period, production of steel dropped from 4.3 million tons (4 million metric tons) to 0.2 million tons (0.18 million metric tons).

In March 1921, Lenin put into effect his New Economic Policy (NEP). An important part of that policy was encouraging peasants to grow more food by allowing them to sell their crop surpluses in private markets for a profit. The central government would no longer seize grain from the peasants but would collect a tax on a fixed percentage of agricultural production. Under the NEP, service businesses and small industries were no longer under state control. They were allowed to hire workers and sell what they produced.

Middlemen—independent private traders known as NEPmen— appeared. They bought and sold goods for high profits. This meant that some aspects of capitalism were now part of the economy. But the government controlled major industries such as coal and iron production, transportation, banks, and foreign trade. Nikolai Bukharin, an economist with the Communist Party, explained:

> In these so-called mixed enterprises part of the shares belong to the Government; the other part may belong to foreign or Russian owners. It is perfectly clear that such mixed enterprises are neither state industries nor purely capitalist industries. Both capitalists and the Workers' Government own stock in them. The Workers' Government receives part of the profits, the private investors receive the remainder. In the course of the future history of such undertakings, there will be a constant struggle between the Government and the private owners to control them. As the proletariat becomes more competent to administer industry, the importance of private ownership will decline. If we make no blunders, the Government will acquire a growing share in these undertakings, in the same way in which, in a capitalist country, great banks and trusts control a vast number of smaller undertakings.

With NEP, agricultural and industrial production, along with the total economy, began to improve, but it came too late to avert catastrophe. Famine and disease threatened large areas of the country.

Drought and Diseases Strike

Even before the NEP was initiated, farm families in the southern regions of Russia had been experiencing the effects of severe drought.

The normal rains didn't come, and crops didn't grow. The government ignored the worsening conditions in the countryside, and officials continued to sell grain to Western countries to gain funds to expand industries.

Farmers who lived in the Volga region knew that their lands were sometimes at risk because of periods of little or no rainfall and winds that blew away dry topsoil. Usually they stored food to last through such times. But government food patrols had taken away their surpluses. When their crops failed in 1920 and 1921, famine was inevitable.

Drought and famine also hit the southern regions of Ukraine, the Urals, the northern Caucasus, the Crimea, and western Siberia. People fled these areas by carts and railroad cattle cars. In a diary entry on August 15, 1921, Alexandra Rakhmanova wrote about this.

CITIZENS IN THE VOLGA REGION CARRY DEAD CHILDREN ON STRETCHERS TO THE CEMETERY, DURING THE FAMINE OF 1920 TO 1921.

The train moves slowly, passing endless evacuation trains from the famine areas of the Volga and the North. The cattle trains are crowded with people, piled up like coal: men, women, children. But are [these] still people? Many of them lost their teeth, their gums are bleeding, their faces are green and ash-gray.

Gruesome accounts of the effects of famine in Russia in 1921 and 1922 fill the pages of numerous books, articles, and newspapers. They tell of people eating rats, cats, dogs, worms, grass, leaves, tree bark, horse manure, dead fish found on riverbanks, anything to fend off hunger. Some reports describe people resorting to cannibalism—eating human flesh. According to historian Orlando Figes, thousands of cases of cannibalism were reported, but most were not made public.

Millions of people died from the famine, as well as from epidemics of diseases such as cholera and typhus. Cholera infections were due primarily to unsanitary living conditions and filthy water supplies.

A Victim of Typhus

A RED ARMY SOLDIER with typhus was captured by the Whites in the last days of the Russian Civil War. He was imprisoned in a typhus barracks. Years later he recalled:

Wherever you looked were spread out the bodies of the sick. . . . Outside, beyond wide-open doors, a sentry patrolled. He didn't let anyone in to us and permitted no one to approach him. . . . The majority of us could not walk: most lay unconscious, others would jump up and step recklessly over the prone bodies of the others. There was an insufferable stench that could be smelled from far away.

Typhus is spread by insects, particularly lice that cover people's bodies and infest straw and other materials used for bedding. The diseases killed more people than the Civil War.

In Moscow, officials frequently denied that a famine existed. But reports from towns and villages in the famine areas described corpses lying in the streets and mass graves of the dead.

Seeking Aid

By the summer of 1921, the evidence of starvation convinced the Communists that they had to ask for foreign aid. Lenin hated the idea of seeking help from capitalists, but he allowed Gorky in July 1921 to appeal to the American Relief Administration (ARA). The ARA had been set up to send aid to Europe after World War I. It was headed by Herbert Hoover, who then was U.S. secretary of commerce. Hoover responded to Gorky's appeal soon after receiving it. His telegram to Gorky was printed in the *New York Times* on July 25. In part it said:

I have read with great feeling your appeal to Americans for charitable assistance to the starving and sick people of Russia, more particularly the children. To the whole American people the absolute sine qua non [essential condition] of any assistance must be the immediate release of the Americans [captured during the Civil War and] now held prisoners in Russia. Once this step has been taken the American Relief Administration, a purely voluntary association . . . together with other cooperating charitable American organizations supported wholly through the generosity of the American people, have funds in hand by which assistance for the children and for the sick could be undertaken immediately.

The Communists agreed to the conditions and released more than one hundred Americans, both citizens and soldiers. After the prisoner release, ARA followed through on its pledge. By mid-1922 it was feeding between ten and eleven million people each day. These efforts—plus medical aid, seed, tools, and clothing—saved millions of lives. Still, more than five million people died between 1920 and 1922 due to starvation and disease. With the famine under control, the ARA halted its operations in 1923.

There was another reason for the ARA to withdraw its aid. Americans were outraged when they discovered that the Communists were

AMERICANS DISTRIBUTE FOOD FROM A RELIEF TRAIN DURING THE 1921 FAMINE.

selling tons of grain to other countries while Russians were starving. U.S. citizens would no longer contribute funds to the ARA for Russian aid.

> *"I have seen people die of hunger. They sit there just waiting to die. I saw one woman with four children all huddling on a single blanket. One of the children died under my own eyes. No one had food to give it."*
>
> —Report on U.S. relief efforts in Russia, *New York Times*, October 24, 1921

The Communists' attitude toward the famine and its victims disturbed many former supporters of the revolution, including Gorky. Over the years following the revolution, Gorky had become as discouraged as Goldman and Berkman. He could not tolerate the lack of human freedom, censorship of writers, and the terror and executions. In October 1921, Gorky left Russia for Italy.

LENIN'S DECLINE

During 1921 Lenin began to show signs of poor health. He complained of headaches and lack of sleep. He was bad tempered and often personally attacked his comrades. Medical experts were unable to diagnose the cause of his illness, other than relating it to exhaustion.

Lenin began to rely on others in the Communist Party to handle daily affairs and paperwork. He turned to Stalin for the most help, appointing him the party's general secretary in April 1922. This position gave Stalin a powerful role in the party. He was already a member of the Politburo—the political section of the Central Committee—and was leader of the Orgburo—the organizational arm—of the party. In these positions, he was able to bring his supporters into the party and recommend thousands of appointments for officials in the provinces.

In May 1922, Lenin suffered a stroke. Although he recovered during the summer, he suffered two more strokes in December. He was partially paralyzed and no longer able to govern. The party was controlled by the Central Committee, but the Politburo appeared before the committee to present views about what policies should be adopted.

VLADIMIR LENIN *(LEFT)* AND JOSEPH STALIN *(RIGHT)* POSE FOR A PICTURE AT GORKI, TWO YEARS BEFORE LENIN'S DEATH.

Members of the Politburo included Lenin, Red Army leader Trotsky, Stalin, Leon Kamenev, and Grigory Zinoviev. Because of Lenin's illness, they all competed with one another for party leadership.

Lenin's health steadily declined, and Stalin convinced the Central Committee that the leader should not be troubled with politics. This would overexcite him and cause his illness to worsen, Stalin said. Lenin was confined to his vacation home at Gorki, named in honor of the famous writer. The Politburo ordered doctors to restrict Lenin's visitors and correspondence.

In late 1922, Lenin began dictating a letter to the Party Congress (a meeting of party leaders), but he ordered that the letter be kept in a sealed envelope until after his death. Lenin was so weak that he could only work for short periods. Dictating the letter took days. It became known later as the Testament. Lenin's secretaries, one of whom was Stalin's wife, Nadezhda, reported the contents of the letter to Stalin.

THE TESTAMENT

In the Testament, Lenin presented his ideas about changes he believed were needed within the party. For one, he advised an increase in the number of Central Committee members. He warned that there was danger of a split in the committee, and that factions could form because of the two leaders Stalin and Trotsky. "I think relations between them make up the greater part of the danger of a split, which could be avoided . . . by increasing the number of C.C. members to 50 or 100," Lenin declared. He added:

Comrade Stalin, having become Secretary-General, has unlimited authority concentrated in his hands, and I am not sure whether he will always be capable of using that authority with sufficient caution. Comrade Trotsky, on the other hand . . . is distinguished not only by outstanding ability. He is personally perhaps the most capable man in the present C.C., but he has displayed excessive self-assurance and shown excessive preoccupation with the purely administrative side of the work.

After dictating this portion of his letter, Lenin learned that, weeks earlier, Stalin had made an abusive telephone call to Nadezhda Krupskaya, Lenin's wife. The call concerned a letter that Lenin had sent to Trotsky. Stalin believed that Lenin and Trotsky were plotting against him. He scolded Krupskaya for disobeying the limit on Lenin's correspondence and threatened to investigate her activities. Lenin was incensed and added another brief note to his Testament. He described Stalin, saying he was:

rude and this defect, although quite tolerable in our midst and in dealing among us Communists, becomes intolerable in a Secretary-General. That is why I suggest that the comrades think about a way of removing Stalin from that post and appointing another man in his stead who in all other respects differs from Comrade Stalin in having only one advantage, namely, that of being more tolerant, more loyal, more polite and more considerate to the comrades.

On January 24, 1924, Lenin died. The political struggle for a new party leader began in earnest. The outcome would determine whether Communist rule would continue as it had in the aftermath of the 1917 revolution or whether it would take a new direction.

CHAPTER 5

Power Struggles

B EFORE AND AFTER LENIN'S DEATH, two basic factions competed for control of the Communist Party: the right
wing and the left wing. Those on the right wanted to continue Lenin's
New Economic Policy and allow peasants to sell their surplus grain.
The left wanted to get rid of the NEP and increase industrialization
while working toward a world revolution.

One of the leaders of the right wing was the economist Nikolai Bukharin. In his view, socialism had to develop gradually. Alexei
Rykov, who had held several commissar positions in the early 1920s,
was allied with Bukharin. So was Mikhail Tomsky, who in 1922 was
elected a member of the Central Committee and Politburo.

On the left were Trotsky, Gregory Zinoviev, and Leon Kamenev.
But the other two had no use for Trotsky. They thought that Trotsky
was arrogant and could not be trusted. Zinoviev and Kamenev formed

FAST FACT

<small>THE SOVIET UNION, OR UNION OF SOVIET SOCIALIST REPUBLICS (USSR), WAS ESTABLISHED IN DECEMBER 1922 BY THE LEADERS OF THE RUSSIAN COMMUNIST PARTY (BOLSHEVIKS). AT THAT TIME, THE NEW NATION INCLUDED THE RUSSIAN, UKRANIAN, BELORUSSIAN, AND TRANSCAUCASIAN REPUBLICS. IN 1956 IT INCLUDED FIFTEEN SEPARATE NATIONS.</small>

an alliance with Stalin to prevent Trotsky from succeeding Lenin. But the alliance was only superficial. Stalin used his authority within the party to undermine Kamenev and Zinoviev as well as Trotsky.

STALIN SCHEMES

Stalin was a grand schemer. As general secretary of the Central Committee and member of the Politburo, he was able to build a strong political power base. He appointed people who were loyal to the party and to him.

While Lenin was in the last stages of his illness, Stalin waited impatiently for him to die. He wanted Lenin out of the way so that he could be in charge. In fact, after Lenin's death, Stalin's secretary reported, "I never saw him [Stalin] in a happier mood . . . satisfaction [was] written all over his face."

Immediately after Lenin died, Stalin arranged funeral plans. He wanted to be seen as loyal to Lenin and his memory. As one of the main speakers at the funeral, Stalin praised Lenin and declared his intention to continue Lenin's revolutionary work. At a congress of the soviets in late January 1924, Stalin declared in a speech:

> Comrades, we Communists are people of a special mould. We are made of a special stuff. We are those who form the army of the great proletarian strategist, the army of Comrade Lenin.

Stalin went on at length to extol the greatness of Lenin. Four times during his speech, he repeated a refrain: "Departing from us, Comrade Lenin enjoined us to hold high and guard the purity of the great title of member of the party, we vow to you, Comrade Lenin, we shall fulfil your behest with honour!"

The congress hoped to rally support for Communism by creating a cult of Lenin—the worship of the leader. They agreed to keep the memory of Lenin alive by changing the name of Petrograd, where the October Revolution began, to Leningrad. They also decided to build a mausoleum, or tomb, of red granite for Lenin in Moscow. Stalin announced that Lenin's body would be embalmed (preserved) and

Embalming Lenin's Body

STALIN INSISTED THAT LENIN'S body be available for public viewing "for posterity." Scientists developed a special embalming procedure and kept it secret for years. First Lenin's organs and brain were removed. Then embalming fluid was injected into Lenin's body. His body then was placed in a chemical bath, said to be a mixture of glycerol and potassium acetate, and checked twice weekly.

In 1991 one of the scientists who attended Lenin's body, Sergei S. Debov, explained that the bath replaced the water in Lenin's skin with the chemical mixture. "The compound has two special qualities. No bacteria grows in it, and just as important, at 16 degrees Celsius [54°F] and 70 percent relative humidity, it does not absorb water or evaporate. So long as we maintain these conditions, the skin remains supple."

Lenin's body is in a glass coffin and can be viewed at his mausoleum, near Red Square in Moscow. Since 1991, when the Soviet Union disbanded, there has been considerable controversy in Russia over whether to continue to display Lenin's body or to bury it in a cemetery, as he had wished. As of 2008, Lenin's embalmed body was still on display.

kept in a glass-covered coffin in the mausoleum, which would become a shrine to the former leader. People would be able to visit and view Lenin's body for years to come. Communist party members used the slogan "Lenin lived, Lenin lives, Lenin will live" to show reverence for Lenin, who became saintlike after his death.

It was Stalin's plan to portray himself as the person who could best carry on after Lenin. But each left-wing and right-wing leader tried to boost his own leadership qualifications by presenting Lenin's ideals to the public.

FAST FACT

A "PERSONALITY CULT" DEVELOPS WHEN A NATION'S LEADER AND FOLLOWERS USE MAGAZINES, NEWSPAPERS, POSTERS, RADIO, AND OTHER MEDIA TO CREATE A HEROIC IMAGE OF THE LEADER. THROUGH FLATTERY AND PRAISE, A LEADER BECOMES A GODLIKE FIGURE TO THE PUBLIC, AS WAS THE CASE WITH LENIN AND STALIN.

Stalin had to find a way to overcome the criticism of him in Lenin's Testament. According to Lenin's instructions, his widow sent the Testament to the Thirteenth Party Congress, held in 1924. It was read before the Central Committee but not the whole congress. Stalin's secretary observed that afterward, "Painful embarrassment paralyzed the whole gathering. Stalin...felt small and miserable. Despite his self-control and forced calm, one could clearly read in his face the fact that his fate was being decided."

Stalin was saved by Kamenev and Zinoviev. They argued that Lenin's fears about Stalin were not supported by evidence. They claimed that Stalin had been cooperative and should remain in his post as general secretary. When Stalin spoke, he pointed out that Lenin had been very ill, implying that Lenin was not thinking clearly when he dictated the Testament. Stalin offered to resign, but the committee would not accept his resignation. So he remained as general secretary and continued to increase his power base.

TROTSKY: STALIN'S RIVAL

Trotsky was Stalin's major rival. The two were opposites in many ways. Trotsky had gained fame for his military skills and his leadership of the Red Army during the Civil War. He was an intellectual, able to develop theories and policies for the party. He was also a great orator and frequently spoke about the theory of world revolution.

Stalin, on the other hand, was completely absorbed in his work as administrator and manipulator of the party. He was also editor of *Pravda*, the party's newspaper. He had none of Trotsky's skills, but he knew very well how to work behind the scenes to plot against his rivals.

One of Stalin's schemes was to appear outwardly friendly toward Trotsky and to convince Zinoviev and Kamenev quietly that they should attack Trotsky as their opponent. Another tactic Stalin used was to declare that Trotsky had not been part of the original group that planned the October Revolution. Repeated numerous times, the lie became accepted as fact.

Stalin also challenged Trotsky's ideas on world revolution. Trotsky (along with Lenin) knew that Russia did not have enough industrial workers to bring about a worldwide proletarian revolution on its own. But by encouraging worker revolutions in other nations, Trotsky thought, Russia's plan for revolution would succeed. Russian efforts to promote world revolution had failed, however. Thus Stalin presented the theory of Socialism in One Country. He was convinced that socialism could develop in a single country—Russia—first and then later be spread internationally.

Socialism in One Country

AFTER LENIN'S DEATH IN 1924, Stalin introduced his political theory of Socialism in One Country. According to the *Encyclopedia of Marxism,* "The theory was in direct opposition to the Bolshevik theory that the success of the Russian Revolution depended on proletarian revolutions in Europe." Stalin insisted that a socialist society could develop inside a single country. His theory became a program of the international Communist organization called Comintern.

Stalin's attacks continued. He accused Trotsky of creating a faction within the party and advocating his own policies rather than Lenin's. Trotsky had few supporters in the Central Committee, and in January 1925 he was forced to give up his post as Commissar of War. Zinoviev and Kamenev tried to get Trotsky kicked out of the party, but Stalin, wanting to appear to be the mediator, opposed such a move. Trotsky remained a member of the Politburo, but he stayed in the background. Historians have wondered why he did not use the Red Army to defend himself, but Trotsky believed that loyalty to the party came first. What the party decided, he accepted.

Stalin waited two more years—until 1927. Then he and the rightist Bukharin pushed Trotsky from the party. Trotsky was exiled in 1928 to Kazakhstan, near the Chinese border. Later, he was deported and lived first in Turkey, then in France, and then Norway. Eventually he and his family found refuge in Mexico, where assassins murdered him in 1940, possibly on orders from Stalin.

Following Trotsky's ejection from the party in 1927, Stalin turned his attention to removing others who had been Lenin's original supporters (known as Old Bolsheviks). By the end of 1929, Kamenev, Zinoviev,

Bukharin, Rykov, and Tomsky were gone from the government. Stalin had replaced them with men loyal to him and his programs.

> *"For forty-three years of my conscious life I have remained a revolutionist. . . . If I had to begin all over again . . . the main course of my life would remain unchanged. . . . My faith in the Communist future of mankind is . . . firmer today, than it was in the days of my youth."*
> —Leon Trotsky, 1940

COLLECTIVIZATION

In 1928 Stalin ended the New Economic Policy. The NEP gave way to Stalin's five-year plan designed to increase production in industry and agriculture. Under this plan, surplus agricultural products would be sold to fund industrialization. To bring about surpluses, Stalin instituted collectivized agriculture. That is, peasants would no longer manage their own village mirs. Traditionally, the village commune elected its own officials and controlled the community's farmland. Village officials also distributed the land according to the size of each household.

With collectivization, peasant communes were forced to give up their land, farm animals, and tools to a large government-run collective farm—a kolkhoz. The central government in Moscow determined what crops and how much of them would be produced on these farms. The government also set the amount that peasants would be paid for their work, set quotas for the share of crops that would be sold to Moscow, and set the prices. Stalin declared these government farms would increase agricultural production so that more grain could be sold, providing income for the development of more industries. As he pointed out in a talk to university students in 1928:

> Large farms are able to employ machines, scientific methods, fertilizers, to increase the productivity of labour, and thus to produce the maximum quantity of marketable grain. On the other hand, the weakness of small-peasant farming lies in the fact that it lacks, or almost lacks, these opportunities, and as a result it is . . . yielding little marketable grain.

Stalin also argued that collectivization would need fewer peasants for farming, so they could work in industry instead. In addition, he declared that poor peasants would no longer be exploited by kulaks. Yet, as was the case when NEP was in force, poor peasants often found work as part-time laborers on kulak farms, mainly farms of 20 acres (8 hectares) or larger. Poor peasants also received help from their wealthier kulak neighbors when there were meager harvests.

KULAK HATRED

Like Lenin, Stalin considered kulaks to be capitalists and enemies of communism. The party spread propaganda that spitefully described kulaks as "vermin," "repulsive," "untouchables," "not human," and "lower than a louse." Many times Stalin made it clear that collectivization would eliminate "the kulaks as a class." By 1930 more than fourteen million peasant households had been forced into collective farms.

Maria Belskia was part of a family of thirteen children when collectivization began. The family joined a kolkhoz, and both her father and mother were hardworking members. They were able to obtain a few farm animals, clothing, and other needed items. Because Maria's parents had a few more material goods than others in the collective, the Communist chairman of the kolkhoz labeled Maria's father a kulak. Even though her father was a loyal Communist, he was expelled from the kolkhoz and jailed. Then her mother was expelled.

The family, like many others, suffered greatly. Communist officials took their small house and belongings, and the family was forced to find shelter in barns or abandoned shacks in the middle of winter. They constantly scrounged for food. Years later Belskia summed up their experience:

> Together and separately, we starved, walked barefoot in the snow, came down with typhoid and malaria, went blind from exhaustion, suffered from whooping cough and tuberculosis, and went mad. None of us got an education. . . . Our childhood was poisoned and taken away from us. . . . We were despised, distrusted, and kept out of all sorts of places. And what was it all for?

Most peasants, kulaks or not, opposed collectivization. They resisted by destroying their livestock and crops or refusing to plant or harvest their fields. Stalin forcibly removed peasants who opposed the program, driving out millions. Some historians estimate that more than fifteen million people were relocated. Two million were made to work as slave laborers on industrial projects. The rest were sent to desolate Siberian regions, where survival was barely possible.

The collectivization of the early 1930s did not bring about increased production. Some of the best farmers had been banished. The farmers who remained neglected livestock and crops. Peasants in the collectives had little reason to produce. They received less for their labor than they had from their communal farms. The foodstuffs they did grow were taken by the government's secret police.

INDUSTRIALIZATION SURGES

Meanwhile, industrialization was proceeding at a fast pace. Stalin nationalized all industries and services. The state set quotas for production and pressed workers to increase the output of manufactured goods.

Iron and steel production and electrical works were top priorities. The manufacture of tractors and other farm machinery, equipment to mechanize the timber and building industries, and coal mining advanced rapidly. So did railroad construction. Much of the increased

> *"We are fifty or one hundred years behind the advanced countries. We must make good this distance in ten years. Either we do it, or we shall go under!"*
>
> —Joseph Stalin, 1931

industrial output was due to millions of peasants who relocated to urban areas to work in factories and to dedicated Communists like Tatiana Fedorova, a Soviet construction worker.

In the 1930s, Fedorova worked on the railway system in underground tunnels. She recalled in an interview for a television series called *People's Century* that young people were enthusiastic about their jobs. In her words:

> We wanted to do something with our own hands, to glorify our country—not just with words but with deeds. And we did it . . . we built the railway. . . .
>
> Everyone was trying to do the best for the country, to raise the heights of the motherland. . . . We worked in such a friendly way. It was such a good time. There wasn't so much to eat, we weren't well dressed. We were simply very happy. Happy because we were making it our personal contribution. If I come to a [railway] station that I was lucky enough to build, it's a bit like meeting my youth when I go there. I'm simply happy that in those years I chose that hard path.

Another supporter was Mary Mackler Leder, an American and the only child of a Jewish family. Her parents were socialists and had emigrated from the United States to the Soviet Union in 1931 during the Great Depression. Her father was prompted by the Soviet promise of a socialist Jewish homeland in Birobidzhan, a region in eastern Russia, close to the Chinese border. The Soviet government set up this autonomous region for Jews escaping persecution in the Crimea and Ukraine, as well as for Jewish immigrants. The family arrived in Birobidzhan and was assigned to a commune. It was a harsh region with severe winters, poor roads, swampy land, no indoor plumbing, and, more important, no place for Mackler to finish high school.

Mary Mackler insisted on going to Moscow, an eleven-day train trip from Birobidzhan on the Trans-Siberian Railroad. At the age of sixteen, her parents allowed her to leave. They believed that "nothing bad could happen to you in a socialist country." She joined an urban commune and became a Communist factory worker in Moscow. Her parents eventually left Birobidzhan because of the difficult conditions and their bitter disappointment in the inefficient and corrupt management of their commune. They returned to the United States in 1933.

Mary Mackler attended Moscow University and became a member of the Komsomol, a Communist youth organization. She married Abram Leder, a fellow Komsomol member who also served in the Red Army. Mary Mackler Leder's story, *My Life in Stalinist Russia*, covers her thirty-four years in Soviet Russia. At first, she was a true believer in Soviet socialism. Leder remained faithful to communist ideals until after World War II (1939–1945), when anti-Semitic (anti-Jewish) attacks, often government supported, became increasingly common. As she put it:

Anti-Semitism . . . existed before and after the revolution. Some of us thought it had been eliminated by the Soviet government's policies . . . that gave Jews equal rights to jobs and education. We found, to our distress, that it had been there all along, merely latent, ready to raise its head at the first opportunity.

Leder attempted to leave the Soviet Union after her husband died in 1959 but repeatedly was denied permission. She finally was able to return to the United States in 1965.

FAMINE AND STARVATION

As the worker populations grew in the urban areas, more food was needed in the cities and manufacturing centers. But the collective farms were not producing enough to meet the demands. Conditions became worse when major famines developed in 1932 and 1933.

Famine hit hardest in Ukraine, where for centuries Ukrainian farmers had owned their own land. Collectivization was an alien concept to them. Communists forced more than 75 percent of Ukrainian farms to be collectivized in 1932. Ukrainians resisted by slaughtering much of their livestock before joining a collective farm.

In 1932 a drought in Ukraine cut crop yields, but Stalin insisted there were no crop failures. He ordered an increase in quotas from the collectives. Grain taken from Ukraine was sold to European markets. Stalin sent Red soldiers to Ukraine to search for any hidden

A UKRAINIAN FAMILY SUFFERS FROM STARVATION DURING THE FAMINE OF 1932 TO 1933.

foodstuffs or animals. One woman, Alisa Maslo, recalled how the food patrols worked:

> [They] took away everything to the last grain . . . they left the family to certain famine death. And so my grandma died and then one of my brothers. . . . My mother was lying in bed swollen with hunger . . . my other brother died. . . . Up came the cart and the man took my brother and dragged him to the cart, and then my own *live* mother. I started crying and the man said, "Go to the orphanage where at least you'll get some soup. She will die anyway, why should I come back a second time?" And so I became an orphan.

Starving people caught taking a few onions or small amounts of wheat or ears of corn from fields were executed or sent to prison. Again, some were so hungry that they resorted to cannibalism, killing and eating members of their own families. Droves of peasants left the countryside and went to urban areas to beg for food, but soldiers would not let them enter the towns.

MILLIONS DIE

As the famine continued into 1933, up to thirty thousand people died each day in Ukraine. The famine also ravaged populations in the Volga and Caucasus regions. Between 1932 and 1933, an estimated five to eight million people died in what many historians have called a human-made famine.

When some Communist leaders witnessed the horrors of the famine, they reported their findings to Stalin. He shrugged off these reports as made-up tales and banned any talk about a famine. Just mentioning the famine could bring a prison sentence or execution. But Stalin's wife, Nadezhda, apparently was not afraid to speak out.

Nadezhda was Stalin's second wife. (His first wife Ekaterina died after two years of marriage.) Called Nadya, she was twenty years younger than Stalin and independent. She learned about the famine from students at an industrial academy where she was taking classes. When she confronted Stalin about this, the two had a fierce argument. The students who spoke to Nadya were arrested, and Stalin ordered her to drop out of classes. Not long afterward, Stalin and Nadya were guests at a banquet and Stalin publicly ridiculed her. She angrily left the dinner, went home, and shot herself. Her housekeeper found her dead in a pool of blood the next morning.

Years later, Stalin's daughter Svetlana explained that her mother was opposed to collectivization and other Stalinist policies. "She really spoke out. My father thought that she was probably on the side of the opposition . . . supporting them against him." Svetlana also reported that Stalin went to view Nadya's coffin and turned from it, saying, "'She went away as an enemy.' . . . He didn't go to the funeral and never visited the cemetery."

Stalin obviously was bitter about his wife's opposition. He also suspected that many in the party were disloyal and trying to undermine his authority. He was determined that nothing would stop him from creating his own kind of revolution. Stalin, as head of a totalitarian government—a government in which only one party rules—would accept nothing less than absolute power. The Russian people were required to be loyal to Stalin and his Communist government. He planned to transform the Soviet Union into an industrialized state, no matter what the cost in lives.

CHAPTER 6

Fear and Terror

I N 1934 THE DROUGHTS were over and the famine eased. Russians began to believe that the promises of the revolution were finally going to be fulfilled. Peasants in collectives were able to bring in a good harvest and relieve hunger in the countryside and urban areas. More than a decade after the revolution, it seemed the stage was set for a better future.

In the towns and cities, Russians saw some signs of progress: new factories and increased industrial production. Farmers and workers began displaying pictures of Stalin and Lenin, glorifying them as heroes. Professionals such as teachers, engineers, and doctors were convinced that the country was being unified.

Russians also compared the economic successes of their five-year plan for industrialization to the plight of people in Western nations who were then suffering from the Great Depression. Businesses in the United States and Europe had failed, banks had closed, and millions of people were jobless, homeless, and penniless. In the United States, private and community organizations provided food at breadlines and soup kitchens.

With the apparent economic progress in the Soviet Union, Communist Party leaders began to suggest that the brutal collectivization methods were no longer needed. Some party members wanted to follow through on Lenin's Testament, replacing Stalin with a more tolerant leader. Opponents thought that Stalin was too radical. They were secretly talking about replacing Stalin and proposed that Sergei Kirov take the job as general secretary.

KIROV SACRIFICED

Kirov was a member of the Politburo and leader of the Leningrad Soviet. He was a close friend of Stalin's and highly respected in Leningrad. Kirov told Stalin about the proposal to replace him. The very idea prompted Stalin to resort to one of his many schemes.

Stalin already was upset with Kirov. Kirov had befriended some of the Old Bolsheviks from Lenin's time and requested that they be brought back into the party. Another source of irritation was that Kirov was building a power base in Leningrad as head of the Leningrad Soviet. In an attempt to diminish Kirov's influence, Stalin in 1933 and 1934 asked Kirov to leave Leningrad and come to Moscow to work. Kirov refused both times.

About the middle of 1934, Stalin decided a purge of the Leningrad Soviet was necessary. Purges, or the "cleaning out" of people suspected of disloyalty, were common during the time of the czars and after the revolution. Stalin's purge would begin with the murder of his good friend.

On December 1, 1934, Kirov was on his way to the Leningrad party headquarters at the Smolny Institute. He and his bodyguard were stopped at the door by the secret police, renamed the People's Commissariat of Internal Affairs, or in NKVD in the Russian initials. The bodyguard was detained, while Kirov started for his office. A young man, Leonid Nikolaev, had been waiting for hours in the dark hallway. He fired his revolver, killing Kirov instantly. Evidence made available only in the 1980s shows that Stalin and the NKVD conspired to carry out the murder, although Stalin was never found directly responsible. Nevertheless, Nikita Khrushchev, one of Stalin's comrades and later the leader of the Communist Party, had "no doubt that Stalin was behind the plot." He recalled that "Kirov was very popular with the party and the people." According to Khrushchev:

[A] blow against Kirov would hurt the party and the people. That's probably why Kirov was marked for sacrifice: his death provided a pretext for shaking up the country and getting rid of undesirables who were out of favor with Stalin. How to get rid of them? By calling them "enemies of the People" and accusing them of "raising their hands against Kirov." . . . Kirov's death was needed for Stalin to take the law into his own hands and crush the Old Bolsheviks.

In short, Kirov's death was Stalin's excuse to start a purge of people opposed to his policies. Stalin had created a totalitarian government. In the Soviet Union, the Communist Party and Stalin had absolute power. The people were required to be loyal to Stalin and his Communist government, which controlled every aspect of people's lives.

The Great Terror

On the same day as Kirov's murder, Stalin issued a decree known as the Law of 1 December. He ordered an investigation of terrorists or anyone suspected of terrorism against Communist officials. Again, he was following a practice established in the aftermath of the revolution. Those arrested were to be tried quickly without legal counsel and with no chance of appeal or pardons. The decree ordered immediate execution of those receiving death sentences.

Some of the first victims were the assassin Leonid Nikolaev, his wife, and several of his relatives, all of whom were executed at the end of December. Others arrested included Zinoviev and Kamenev—who were accused of conspiring to overthrow Stalin—and members of the right-wing opposition, such as Bukharin and Rykov. Within months after Kirov's murder, tens of thousands were arrested and charged with being enemies of the people.

Stalin set quotas for the number of arrests and executions to be carried out by the NKVD and local police. People could be arrested for minor offenses, such as making a mistake at work, telling a joke unfavorable to Stalin, having relatives opposed to the regime, or talking in a hostile way about the party. People from all backgrounds—officers in the Red Army, NKVD officials, priests, artists, writers, people who had spent time in other countries, children of suspects, and non-Russian nationalities such as Ukrainians—were purged. The purge of the Red Army brought death to more than thirty-eight thousand army officers. Three thousand sailors and officers in the Russian fleet also were executed.

Members of Stalin's extended family were not spared. Among those arrested was the godfather of his mother-in-law, Abel

Yenukidze. As Svetlana noted, "My father had known Abel Yenukidze for ages. . . . Although he was not a big shot, he was well known, he had worked for Lenin, was quite high in the Party hierarchy—and yet he was a victim."

Stalin systematically eliminated his "enemies"—known or suspected. People became suspicious of each other and constantly feared that someone, out of jealousy or hatred, would label them for arrest. "Any adult inhabitant of this country, from a collective farmer up to a member of the Politburo, always knew that it would take only one careless word or gesture and he would fly off" never to be seen again, wrote author and dissident Aleksandr Solzhenitsyn, who was held in one of Stalin's forced-labor camps.

In many cases, those arrested were tortured to gain confessions about their supposed crimes. The secret police often threatened to torture or kill prisoners' family members to get them to confess.

Millions of prisoners were sentenced to death, several thousand on one day alone. Those sent to forced-labor camps were taken to one of hundreds of locations across the Soviet Union, many of them in icy Siberia. This network of camps is known as the Gulag, which stands for Glavnoe Upravlenie Lagerei, or Main Camp Administration.

Prisoners sent to remote areas were transported by freight cars on slow-moving trains that stopped only every few days to get water for the engine's boiler. One victim recalled, "What they gave us to eat was salted fish. And they gave us nothing to drink." The salted fish, usually herring, made the prisoners thirstier than they already were. But they had to eat the fish or starve.

At these camps, only the strong were able to survive, especially in the frigid weather of the arctic winter. As one survivor said, "They didn't need gas chambers because the frost finished you off." People

Forced to Build a Canal

HUNDREDS OF THOUSANDS OF men and women in forced-labor camps built the Belomor Canal, a ship canal, during the 1930s. Also called the White Sea–Baltic Sea Canal, it joined the two northern seas and was meant to transport Russia's naval fleet. Construction of the canal probably cost tens of thousands of lives. The canal was abandoned in the 1960s because it was too shallow for most ships.

were forced to work in all kinds of jobs, such as logging, mining, fishing, building canals, constructing factories, and manufacturing military equipment. The long hours, brutal work, and lack of adequate food and clothing killed up to 8 million people between 1936 and 1938. Robert Conquest, a U.S. researcher of Soviet history, estimates that only 10 percent of camp prisoners survived. About 2 million prisoners were in the Gulag system at any given time during the thirty years of Stalin's rule.

SHOW TRIALS

In 1936 Stalin initiated a series of show trials, or sham trials without any elements of justice or fairness. The prisoner on trial makes a public confession, and the verdict is already determined. In these trials from 1936 to 1938, Stalin's political opponents publicly confessed to trumped-up charges of treason, sabotage, or other crimes against the nation, after months of imprisonment in crowded cells without proper food and enduring all kinds of torture. Among those found guilty and sentenced to death were Kamenev, Zinoviev, Rykov, and Bukharin. Trotsky also received a death sentence, even though he was in exile at the time. Rykov attempted to save his life by writing to the Supreme Soviet of the Soviet Union:

On March 13 [1938] the Military Tribunal of the Supreme Court condemned me to death by shooting. I ask for clemency [mercy].

My guilt before the party and the country is great, but I have a passionate desire and, I think, enough strength to expiate [make up for] it.

I ask you to believe that I am not a completely corrupt person. In my life there were many years of noble, honest work for the revolution. I can still prove that even after having committed so many crimes, it is possible to become an honest person and to die with honor.

I ask that you spare my life.

March 13, 1938

[signed] A. I. Rykov

Rykov's appeal did him no good. He was shot to death along with the other "traitors." Secret police records show that during 1938, at least 350,000 people were shot. But researchers estimate that the figure could be as high as 1.5 million executed that year. Included among those shot to death were members of the Central Committee. According to the PBS television program *Red Files*, "As of 1939, only 31 of 139 Central Committee members from 1934 remained alive."

In Stalin's Image

While Stalin's purges created fear throughout the land and solidified his power, censorship and propaganda influenced people's thinking and provided reasons for them to believe in his authority. Only positive images of Stalin were allowed. Anything depicting Stalin in a negative manner was altered. In speeches, publications, and other media, Stalin was described in phrases such as "supreme genius of humanity," "leader of genius of the toilers of the whole world," and "inspirer and organizer of the victory of socialism."

IN THE 1930S, IMAGES OF STALIN AND LENIN HUNG EVERYWHERE IN RUSSIA, INCLUDING THIS FACTORY.

Photographs, statues, and posters showing Stalin as a lover of children, as a military hero, or as a godlike figure were everywhere. One poster depicted smiling children greeting Stalin with flowers. The caption read, "Thank you, our dear Stalin, for our happy childhood!" Those words became a mocking and bitter catchphrase for families driven from their homes during purges.

"[Stalin] was great as a thinker and as someone who acts. He was also a good person. . . . He deserves a good word despite all the things that are said about him; he deserves good words. He united people."
—Tatiana Fedorova, Soviet construction worker, 1934

Line drawings or photographs in publications frequently showed Stalin in an imperial pose with his arm inside his jacket. The pose mirrored paintings of Napoleon Bonaparte, a general in the French Revolution (1779–1789), who later became France's emperor. Some images depicted Stalin with Lenin's name on a banner in the background, a way to show Stalin as Lenin's rightful successor. In addition, paintings and drawings showed farmers bringing in plentiful harvests and workers toiling with great energy. Such images also appeared in Soviet films. An American professor of European history, Steven Kreis, described one movie:

[It] showed thousands of collective farmers having a gargantuan feast against the backdrop of a new power station. Recently I had a talk with its producer, [a] gifted and intelligent man.

"How could you produce such a film?" I asked. . . . The producer smiled a sad smile. "You know, the strangest thing to me is that I was absolutely sincere. I thought all this was a necessary part of building communism. And then I believed Stalin."

MEDIA PROPAGANDA

Films were an important element in Stalin's propaganda machine. As Stalin wrote in a letter to a comrade in 1935, "Possessing exceptional possibilities of cultural influence on the masses, the cinema helps the working class and its party to educate the workers in the spirit of socialism, to organize the masses in the struggle for socialism, to heighten their sense of culture and political awareness." Stalin wrote that he expected films to glorify "the grandeur of historical achievements in the struggle of the workers and peasants for power in the Soviet Union, mobilizing them in order to accomplish new tasks and reviewing not only the successes but also pointing out the difficulties in socialist construction."

Literature played another important role in Stalin's propaganda. He established the Writers' Union to oversee what was written. If an author's work did not suit Stalin, she or he was likely to be labeled an enemy and sent to the Gulag. Authors, poets, and playwrights were required to praise Stalin in their writings. Russian history texts were written to extol Stalin's role in the revolution. A primary example is Emelyan Yaroslavsky's 1938 *History of the Communist Party of the Soviet Union (Bolsheviks): Short Course.* In the text, Stalin is credited with organizing the 1917 revolution and suppressing opponents. The *Short Course* became a bible for Stalinists—his loyal followers and those who claimed to be supporters. More than forty million copies of the book were published worldwide. Officials censored other history books and changed them to state that Stalin was a hero of the revolution. They removed the names of the other Bolsheviks who planned the uprising.

Hymns, poems, and speeches spoke of Stalin as a great leader, educator, and father figure. The writer A. O. Avdienko praised Stalin at a Writers' Union meeting:

> The men of all ages will call on thy name, which is strong, beautiful, wise and marvelous. Thy name is engraven on every factory, every machine, every place on the earth, and in the hearts of all men. . . . I shall be eternally happy and joyous, all thanks to thee, great educator, Stalin. Everything belongs to thee, chief of our great country. And when the woman I love presents me with a child the first word it shall utter will be: Stalin.

Cities, town squares, streets, and buildings were named for Stalin. The city of Tsaritsyn in southeastern Russia was renamed Stalingrad. Azerbaijani poet and playwright Vagif Samadoghlu explained in a 1999 essay:

> As difficult as it is to comprehend today, many people living in the Soviet Union absolutely worshipped Stalin despite the fact that millions lost their lives because of him. They saw him as their protector. It's only natural that every human being has an intense need to feel secure. But those who understood Stalin's true nature—usually those who were more urbanized—either became victims of his repressive leadership and were killed or exiled, or they learned to keep silent.

Foreign Approval of the Soviet System

At the time of Stalin worship in the Soviet Union, Western countries, including Great Britain, France, Germany, and the United States, contained many Soviet supporters. During the 1920s and 1930s, communism and its leaders were popular among many American artists, writers, filmmakers, intellectuals, and members of the labor movement. They saw communism as a way to help the poor, especially after the Depression. Tens of thousands of these Western professionals visited Russia during the 1920s and 1930s. These visitors were escorted on tours of Russia by the All-Union Society for Cultural Relations with Foreign Countries (VOKS). VOKS tours allowed visitors to view only favorable aspects of Russian life.

Among the foreign visitors was the famed Irish playwright George Bernard Shaw, a dedicated socialist who supported Stalin and his programs. When asked about the purges and execution of the Old Bolsheviks of the 1917 revolution, Shaw responded, "They often have to be pushed off the ladder with a rope around their necks."

British biologist Julian Huxley was another who could see or hear no evil about Stalin. Huxley visited Russia in the 1930s and reported that there was no such thing as a famine in the countryside. The American author Theodore Dreiser, who was a committed socialist, also wrote and spoke favorably about Stalin and the Soviet Union. However, many Americans who supported socialism or communism became disenchanted when they learned the truth about Stalin's dictatorship and the deaths of millions in the Soviet Union.

CHAPTER 7

The Soviet Union Faces the World

AFTER THE 1917 REVOLUTION, the Soviets had to concentrate immediately on internal conflicts and chose to withdraw from international affairs. But during the 1930s, Stalin began to be wary of possible threats to the Soviet Union from foreign enemies. He kept track of international relations through Comintern, based in Moscow, the organization that sought to establish communism worldwide. Comintern members in various countries provided information to Stalin that in some cases prompted Soviet intervention in other nation's affairs.

China is an example. In 1936 two major political parties in China, the Nationalists and Communists, were engaged in a civil war. At the same time, Japan was threatening China. Japan also had clashed with Russia over control of Manchuria on the Chinese-Russian border and Port Arthur in southern Manchuria. Stalin knew that a unified China could forcefully oppose Japan. He urged Nationalist leader Chiang Kai-chek and Communist leader Mao Zedong to unite their forces against the Japanese.

> *"The Communist Party of the Soviet Union is our best teacher and we must learn from it."*
> —Mao Zedong, China's Communist leader, 1949

However, stopping Japanese aggression was not a priority for Chiang Kai-chek. He knew that his armies could not win against the more powerful and better-armed Japanese forces. He was determined to destroy the Communists first, then unite the country and face the Japanese.

Stalin, through his Comintern adviser in China, continued to push for Chinese unity. Although neither side was eager to comply, the Nationalists and Communists did form a united front when Japan invaded China in 1937. But they did not join forces. Each side agreed to a defined area where it would fight the Japanese. During the fighting, the Communists had more success than the Nationalists in holding territory, due in part to the military equipment and funds that Stalin supplied.

A Pact with the Nazis

While Stalin intervened in China, the Soviet Union faced threats of a possible German invasion on its western border. By the mid-1930s, the German dictator Adolf Hitler, leader of the Nazi Party, had already expanded German territory with the occupation of the Rhineland to the west. In the east, Germany occupied the Sudetenland, a part of Czechoslovakia that had been taken from Germany by the Versailles Treaty at the end of World War I. In 1936 Stalin signed an economic agreement with Germany to stay on good terms with the aggressive Hitler. Germany moved into Austria in 1938 and into the rest of Czechoslovakia in 1939. That year Stalin proposed an alliance with Great Britain and France. He believed that such an alliance would prevent a German attack, because Hitler would not want to risk a war with other Western nations.

But British prime minister Neville Chamberlain believed in a policy called appeasement. He would compromise with an aggressor such as Hitler in order to keep the peace. Many British did not want to risk a war, and some believed that a strong Germany would prevent Communist Russia from gaining more power.

On March 26, 1939, Chamberlain wrote to a friend, "I must confess to the most profound distrust of Russia. . . . I distrust her motives, which seem to me to have little connection with our ideas of liberty, and to be concerned only with getting everyone else by the ears."

When the British rejected the alliance, Stalin suspected that Great Britain was going to join Germany in a plot to invade the USSR. He and foreign minister Vyacheslav Molotov decided to make overtures to Hitler. With Hitler's approval, Germany's foreign minister Joachim von Ribbentrop contacted Molotov and arranged for a meeting in Moscow during the summer of 1939.

The two dictators had their own reasons for putting aside their differences. Hitler was preparing to invade Poland and did not want the USSR to oppose him. Stalin, for his part, wanted to extend Soviet territory in the west to protect its border while at the same time avoiding a war.

Ribbentrop arrived in Moscow on August 19, 1939, to work out two pacts. The first was an economic agreement in which the USSR promised to provide food and raw materials, such as oil and cotton, to Germany. In exchange, Germany promised to provide the USSR with manufactured products such as machinery and military supplies.

Four days later, on the afternoon of August 23, the two foreign ministers met again. After a long session that lasted into the early hours of August 24, Molotov and Ribbentrop, with Stalin oversee-ing, signed the Nazi-Soviet Pact. The treaty is also known as the

VYACHESLAV MOLOTOV *(SEATED)* SIGNS THE GERMAN-SOVIET NONAGGRESSION PACT ON AUGUST 23, 1939, AS JOACHIM VON RIBBENTROP *(LEFT)* AND JOSEPH STALIN *(CENTER)* LOOK ON.

German–Soviet Nonaggression Pact, Hitler–Stalin Pact, or Molotov–Ribbentrop Pact.

Part of the agreement was a pledge that the Soviet Union and Germany would not attack each other "either individually or jointly with other Powers." A section of the treaty, the "Additional Secret Protocol," allowed the Soviet Union to expand by annexing (taking over) Estonia, Latvia, Lithuania, a portion of Finland on the Baltic Sea, and Bessarabia, an area near the Black Sea, all former parts of the old Russian Empire. The two nations also secretly agreed to divide Poland between them.

"I hope that the German-Soviet Nonaggression Pact will mark a decisive turn for the better in the political relations between our two countries."
—Joseph Stalin, in a 1939 letter to Germany's Adolf Hitler

WORLD WAR II BEGINS

Not long after the treaty was signed, on September 1, 1939, Germany invaded Poland. The invasion was a blitzkrieg, a German word for "lightning war." Planes, tanks, and artillery attacked rapidly at numerous locations. On September 3, Britain and France declared war on Germany. World War II was under way.

The Polish forces tried to defend their nation, but they were overpowered. At the end of September, Poland surrendered, and Germany occupied the western half of the country. In the meantime, while the fighting was still going on, Soviet forces moved into Poland to occupy its eastern half, according to the terms of the secret portion of the Nazi-Soviet Pact.

One after another, the countries of Europe fell to Adolf Hitler and his Nazi military machine. In 1940 Italy and Japan joined Germany to form an alliance known as the Axis. Fighting against the Axis were the Allies, which included Great Britain, France, China, and more than forty other nations.

In early 1941, Stalin received warnings from his intelligence services and even from the Chinese Communist Party that Germany was planning an attack on the Soviet Union. German planes were flying daily over the Soviet Union, but Stalin did not order them shot down for violating Soviet air space. Nor did he allow any anti-German propaganda. Stalin believed Hitler would not betray the Nazi-Soviet Pact. He was also convinced that reports of a German attack were lies coming from the British. He thought the British were trying to divert the Nazis by provoking a war between the Soviet Union and Germany. In Stalin's view, Germany would finish its war with Great Britain before attacking anywhere else.

Germany Attacks the Soviet Union

During the spring of 1941, German troops began to assemble along the western borders of USSR territories. Stalin still did little to mobilize troops. In fact, because of earlier purges of the military, the Red Army had to be rebuilt. There were not enough commanders left to rebuild it.

On June 21, 1941, Nikita Khrushchev, the Communist leader in Ukraine, received a warning from military headquarters in Kiev that the Germans were ready to attack. The next day, June 22, the Germans began a huge military assault. From 3 to 4 million (some reports say more than 4.5 million) German troops invaded the USSR at various points along the borders of the territories that Stalin had obtained through the Nazi–Soviet Pact. The Nazis had thousands of tanks and aircraft to deploy along a 1,500-mile (2,400 km) front, from north to south. Soviet forces numbered about half those of the Nazis, and the Soviets were forced to retreat. The Germany armies killed hundreds of thousands of Soviet soldiers and imprisoned at least that many more. They destroyed more than one thousand Soviet military aircraft.

Stalin could not believe what had happened. According to numerous reports, he did not appear in public for more than a week. He stayed at a dacha, one of his country houses. As Stalin's daughter Svetlana recalled:

> He had believed that the Germans would never attack: "You can trust the Germans, you can trust Hitler. We have a pact. They will attack everybody else, but they will never attack us" [Stalin said]. He just sat there completely depressed, for quite a while. He just couldn't get himself together. It was 22 June when they attacked, and not until 3 July did he speak to the nation.

Stalin broadcast his speech over the radio, addressing his audience as "comrades," "sisters," and "brothers." He called on them to fight the "Great Patriotic War." But the situation was bleak. As Khrushchev declared in his memoir years later:

Our situation was disastrous from the very beginning. Stalin failed to designate which plants should produce rifles, artillery, ammunition, tanks, and armored vehicles, so there simply weren't anywhere near enough weapons.

Khrushchev went to the front lines on the western border of Ukraine with a top military commander, Georgi Zhukov. In his memoir, Khrushchev reported: "We immediately could tell there was a shortage of arms. We had too few planes, too few tanks." Khrushchev made a telephone call to Moscow to request rifles but was told there were none. He was told to manufacture swords and knives and to fill bottles with explosive materials for the troops to use in battle. "The whole thing was a disgrace," Khrushchev wrote.

DEFENDING MAJOR CITIES

In August 1941, the Germans reached Leningrad, surrounded the city, and cut off supply lines. Leningrad was under siege for nine hundred days, trapping 2.5 million people. As the Germans pushed deep into the Soviet Union, U.S. president Franklin D. Roosevelt sent aid to Russia in October 1941. Although the United States was not involved in the war at that time, Roosevelt, along with then British prime minister Winston Churchill, knew that the Soviet Union was vital to winning the war against the Nazis.

Stalin was determined to hold Leningrad, but he also had to save Moscow. The Germans were on their way to attack the capital in October 1941. Stalin concentrated Red Army forces around the outskirts of the capital. In mid-October, he prepared to evacuate Moscow. First he arranged to have the "sacred" body of Lenin moved east of

Moscow to a school in Tyumen, Siberia, where it was under guard day and night. The Lenin mausoleum in Moscow was guarded to give the impression that Lenin was still there.

Stalin moved his family to his dacha at Kuibyshev, a city on the Volga River. He also sent his personal papers and library to the dacha and was ready to go to his secret bunker there. Lavrenti Beria, one of Stalin's closest advisers, ordered party leaders to evacuate everyone who could not fight.

Stalin himself was set to leave Moscow by train, but then he did an abrupt about-face. He decided to stay and show that Moscow would not be taken by the Germans. The Red Army fought the exhausted

CITIZENS OF LENINGRAD GATHER WATER FROM A BROKEN WATER MAIN DURING THE WINTER OF 1942, WHILE THE CITY WAS UNDER SIEGE BY THE GERMAN ARMY.

A Leningrad Eyewitness

DURING WORLD WAR II, the Germans surrounded the city of Leningrad from 1941 to 1944, cutting off food supplies. Each month, thousands died of starvation. Anna Andreievna, manager of a hotel, survived. In an interview with a London *Sunday Times* correspondent, she recalled:

> The city's population of dogs, cats, horses, rats and crows disappeared as they became the main course on many dinner tables. Reports of cannibalism began to appear. Thousands died—an estimated 11,000 in November increasing to 53,000 in December. The frozen earth meant their bodies could not be buried. Corpses accumulated in the city's streets, parks and other open areas.

Germans, who had pushed through snow and ice for more than 500 miles (800 km) to Moscow and defeated them. But by the end of 1941, the war had expanded beyond Europe and Russia.

On December 7, 1941, Japan bombed the U.S. naval base at Pearl Harbor, Hawaii, and the United States joined the Allies in World War II. Roosevelt hoped to arrange a meeting with Stalin to ensure that the Soviets would also enter the war against Japan. Stalin, however, had to deal with threats at home. Hitler planned to attack another major Soviet city—Stalingrad.

Stalingrad (modern Volgograd) is in the middle of the Volga region. If Hitler and his army could control the city, they could cut off Soviet supplies of oil, grain, and potatoes. In the summer of 1942, the Germans attacked Stalingrad. At first it seemed as though the Germans would be successful, but Stalin ordered the Soviet Army to stand

and fight. Battles went on until February 1943, when the Germans finally gave up.

Ending the War

Stalin met with Roosevelt and Churchill in late 1943. The Big Three, as they were called, met at Tehran, Iran. There, the three leaders planned a major offensive in Europe: the western allies would invade France, which had been occupied by the Nazis, while the Soviet Union would launch attacks to drive Axis forces out of Eastern Europe. The invasion was called D-Day and took place on June 6, 1944. By August 5, Allied troops were in Paris, France, to liberate the city. The German Army also finally left Leningrad in 1944, after almost three years of German siege. By the end of 1944, most of the prewar Soviet territory was free of German troops.

Other meetings of the Big Three took place during the war. One crucial conference was held February 4 to February 11, 1945, at Yalta, in southern Russia. The war in Europe appeared to be coming to an end. At the Yalta Conference, Stalin, Roosevelt, and Churchill discussed how to divide Germany once the Nazis had surrendered. They agreed that Germany would be divided among Great Britain, France, the Soviet Union, and the United States. In addition, Roosevelt and Churchill wanted assurances from Stalin that the Soviet Union would support the war in the Pacific against Japan. Stalin agreed to enter that fight after the war in Europe ended. In exchange, Stalin wanted territory in East Asia.

The future of Poland was the most difficult issue. Poland at the time was divided between Germany and the Soviet Union. Stalin wanted to control Poland, but the other two leaders were adamantly opposed. They called for Polish independence. Stalin agreed to free elections in Poland and other Eastern European countries. Although the Yalta conference seemed to end in a friendly manner, there was soon friction between the Soviet Union and the United States.

Germany finally surrendered on May 7, 1945. In July 1945, Harry S. Truman—who became U.S. president when Roosevelt died earlier that year—met in Potsdam, Germany, with Churchill and Stalin. The three leaders discussed how to establish postwar order. At the meeting, Truman revealed that an atomic (or nuclear) bomb had been tested successfully in the United States. The three leaders were confident that the threat of the bomb would bring an end to the war in a very short time. They agreed that a declaration of this news should be issued to Japan.

Later that month, on July 26, 1945, the Potsdam Declaration demanded that Japan surrender or face destruction. Japan ignored the demand. On August 6, 1945, a U.S. bomber, the *Enola Gay*, dropped an atomic bomb on Hiroshima, Japan. It vaporized the city in seventy-five seconds. Three days later, on August 9, the United States dropped a second atomic bomb on Nagasaki, Japan. Finally, on August 14, 1945, Japan surrendered. World War II came to an end.

The War's Aftermath

In late 1945, Stalin became ill. His daughter Svetlana recalled that Stalin "fell apart. . . . But it was kept a state secret—they didn't even tell me at the time. I had no idea what was wrong; I couldn't even get through on the telephone. . . . My father survived but he was never the same again."

Stalin had had a minor stroke, and his left arm was paralyzed. He recuperated at his dacha near the Black Sea for nearly three months, from October to the middle of December. His health improved somewhat, and he returned to Moscow to deal with some of the major problems in the aftermath of the war.

World War II had left a huge number of military and civilian dead and wounded. It had devastated the USSR. More than 27 million Russians died in battle, labor camps, and in shattered cities and villages. German forces had burned more than 1,700 cities and towns and tens of thousands of villages. About 25 million people were homeless. Thousands of factories and collective farms had been destroyed. The loss of livestock, machinery, and farm laborers devastated agriculture.

Rebuilding was, of course, urgent in the Soviet Union as well as in other parts of the world. But there were also political problems. At the end of the war, Western nations at first were sympathetic to the Soviets, but by 1946 they were no longer eager to support them.

In 1944 Stalin had given Beria, as head of the national security agency, control of the Soviet atomic bomb project as well. There was concern in Western nations about how far Stalin would go in developing nuclear arms.

Western nations also feared that Stalin was trying to spread communism throughout Europe. Stalin's actions pointed in that direction. For one thing, he failed to keep pledges he had made to the Allies. He had promised free elections in Poland, but instead he forced a Communist government on the Poles. In addition, the Soviets retained a military hold on other Eastern European countries, including Albania, Bulgaria, Czechoslovakia, East Germany, Hungary, and Romania. The Soviets were pressuring Turkey as well. They wanted military bases in that country in order to have free access to the Mediterranean Sea.

The United States and other Western nations suspected that Stalin

The "Thunder of His Name"

AFTER WORLD WAR II, Stalin continued to present himself, through countless media slogans and images, as the great, godlike Communist leader. According to Russian author and historian Edvard Radzinsky:

> The earth was filled with the thunder of his name. As a contemporary wrote in her diary: "Stalin here, Stalin there, Stalin, Stalin everywhere. You can't go out to the kitchen, or sit on the toilet, or eat without Stalin following you. . . . He creeps into your guts and your very soul, creeps into your brain, stops up all holes, treads on a person's heels, rings you up in your innermost self . . . haunts your memories and your dreams."

When Stalin celebrated his seventieth birthday, in December 1949, there was a grand show at the Bolshoi Theater in Moscow. He was showered with adulation and gifts galore. Even China's Communist leader, Mao Zedong, who had established the People's Republic of China in 1949, attended the celebration.

was planning even further expansion. Winston Churchill, no longer in office, declared in a March 1946 speech at Westminster College in the United States:

> An iron curtain has descended across the [European] Continent. Behind that line lie all the capitals of the ancient states of Central and Eastern Europe . . . and all are subject in one form or another, not only to Soviet influence but to a very high and, in some cases, increasing measure of control from Moscow. . . . The Communist parties, which were very small

in all these Eastern States of Europe, have been raised to pre-eminence and power far beyond their numbers and are seeking everywhere to obtain totalitarian control.

President Truman was in the audience during Churchill's speech (called the Iron Curtain speech). Later, Truman advocated sending financial support to nations trying to be free of Soviet control. In March 1947, he proclaimed the Truman Doctrine, which provided millions of dollars to Greece, Turkey, and other countries to resist the Communists. Stalin was not pleased and never again met with Truman. This was the beginning of a "cold war," a period of tension without actual fighting between the two postwar superpowers, the United States and the Soviet Union.

THE COLD WAR

In 1948 the Cold War almost became a hot war due to the partition of Germany. The British, French, and Americans wanted to combine their occupation areas (the areas each controlled after the war, as agreed at Yalta) into one country, which would eventually become the Federal Republic of Germany, or West Germany. The Soviets were opposed, because they believed this move would lead to a reunified Germany and a loss of Soviet power. Berlin, the capital of Germany, was located in the Soviet-controlled section of the country. It also was divided into four zones. To prevent the formation of West Germany, the Soviet Union in June 1948 blocked traffic going through its section of Germany from reaching the Western-controlled portion of Berlin, thereby cutting off food, fuel, and other necessities.

Truman immediately ordered an American airlift. With the help of the British Royal Air Force, and French and West Berlin leaders, the airlift delivered lifesaving supplies to West Berliners. The Soviet blockade ended in May 1949. Afterward, the eastern zone of Germany, under Communist rule, became known as the German Democratic Republic, or East Germany.

Other events during the Cold War showed the increasing divide between Communist and non-Communist nations. In 1949 the United States, Canada, Great Britain, France, and other Western nations signed a treaty called the North Atlantic Treaty Organization (NATO). The signers agreed to defend each other if attacked by a nonallied country. Over the next few years, other non-Communist Western European countries joined NATO.

In his last years, Stalin did not hesitate to express his hostility toward the West. He supported Communist northern Korea's invasion of southern Korea in 1950. This invasion resulted in a war that lasted for three years.

A PLANE LANDS AT THE BERLIN AIR BASE AS PART OF THE BERLIN AIRLIFT IN 1948.

During the Korean War, the Soviet Union supplied North Korea with tanks, arms, and other materials. Under the sponsorship of the United Nations, the United States and fifteen other nations joined South Koreans in their fight to prevent a Communist takeover. A 1953 agreement divided the country into North Korea and South Korea.

When West Germany joined NATO in 1955, the Soviet Union created the Warsaw Pact, which was signed in Warsaw, Poland. It was a treaty between the USSR and the Eastern European nations under Soviet control. The contracting parties agreed to defend each other and protect each member country's security.

The Warsaw Pact

THE WARSAW PACT, A treaty between the USSR, Albania, Bulgaria, Czechoslovakia, East Germany, Hungary, Poland, and Romania, became effective in 1955. It was a mutual defense treaty. At the time, the Soviet premier was Nikita Khrushchev. In his memoirs, Khrushchev explained reasons for the treaty:

> I think it is important to say that in setting up the pact, we wanted to make an impression on the West. It is safe to say that the time when the West could talk with the Soviet Union and its social- ist allies . . . passed long ago. We formed the Warsaw Pact in response to their formation of NATO.

> Those two forces oppose each other throughout the world. . . . Many times we have officially expressed our willingness to liquidate our Warsaw Pact if the West would liquidate NATO. Because of that it cannot be said that the Warsaw Pact is a preparation for war. It is a preparation for defense in case of war against socialist countries.

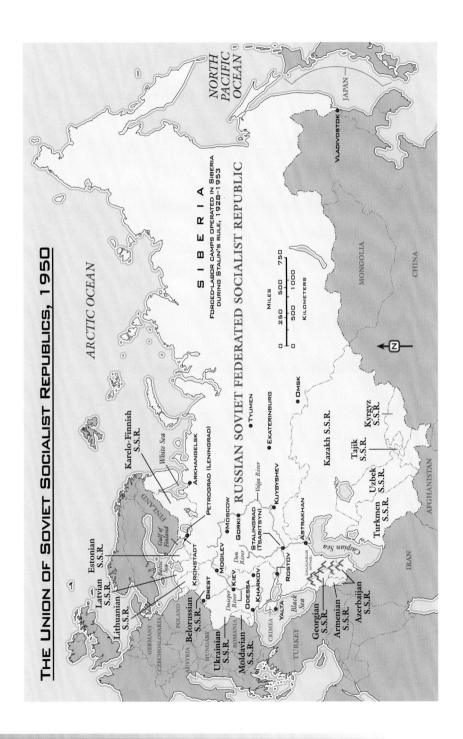

THE UNION OF SOVIET SOCIALIST REPUBLICS, 1950

ARCTIC OCEAN

NORTH PACIFIC OCEAN

SIBERIA

FORCED-LABOR CAMPS OPERATED IN SIBERIA
DURING STALIN'S RULE, 1928–1953

RUSSIAN SOVIET FEDERATED SOCIALIST REPUBLIC

MILES
0   250   500   750
0   500   1000
KILOMETERS

JAPAN

VLADIVOSTOK

MONGOLIA

CHINA

Kazakh S.S.R.

Kyrgyz S.S.R.

Tajik S.S.R.

Uzbek S.S.R.

Turkmen S.S.R.

AFGHANISTAN

IRAN

Caspian Sea

Karelo-Finnish S.S.R.

White Sea

ARKHANGELSK

PETROGRAD (LENINGRAD)

FINLAND

Gulf of Finland

Baltic Sea

Estonian S.S.R.

Latvian S.S.R.

Lithuanian S.S.R.

KRONSTADT

Belorussian S.S.R.

BREST

MOGILEV

KIEV

Dnieper River

ODESSA

KHARKOV

Don River

ROSTOV

CRIMEA

YALTA

Black Sea

MOSCOW

GORKI

STALINGRAD (TSARITSYN)

Volga River

KUYBYSHEV

ASTRAKHAN

CAUCASUS MTNS.

Georgian S.S.R.

Armenian S.S.R.

Azerbaijan S.S.R.

TURKEY

TYUMEN

EKATERINBURG

OMSK

Ukrainian S.S.R.

Moldavian S.S.R.

ROMANIA

HUNGARY

POLAND

CZECHOSLOVAKIA

AUSTRIA

GERMANY

More Purges and Terror

Although Stalin was aging, he still wielded total control over all aspects of life in the Soviet Union. He began to fear that Soviets would be influenced by Western ideas and would rebel. He ordered a new wave of purges and terror, similar to those in the 1930s. It became a crime to praise democracy, especially U.S. democracy. Russian soldiers in World War II who had been prisoners of war had returned home only to be sent to labor camps, because they had seen too much of the West. Purges of military leaders and the intelligentsia (teachers, writers, and others who work with ideas) were common.

By the 1950s, Stalin was seeing enemies everywhere. Some historians report that he became paranoid, or suspicious of everyone. He worked long hours, from late afternoon to the early morning hours of the next day. Afterward he insisted that his comrades join him for dinner.

Khrushchev attended many of those dinners, which he described as "horrible." They did not end until just before breakfast, and guests had to go to work the next day. If there was a dinner that night, Khrushchev reported:

> It always ended badly for anyone who started to doze at Stalin's table. . . . He would throw a tomato at you if you nodded off. I saw it myself during the war years. We would go to the dacha to talk over military matters, and after reports were over, he always invited us to his quarters. Then the dinners would begin.
>
> The dinner would end with fruit being thrown, tomatoes and the like. It got so bad that he would pelt people with forks and spoons.

The dinners, accompanied by crude antics, dirty jokes, and dancing only with other men (since no women were invited), were common affairs during the early 1950s. This was also a time when Stalin published two pamphlets on socialism, exposed those he thought were planning to kill him, and planned another reign of terror.

Stalin also began a campaign called the doctors' plot against Jews. He falsely claimed that Jewish doctors had tried to poison him. He ordered the secret police to arrest and execute or send to the Gulag dozens of Jewish doctors and eventually hundreds of Jewish professionals, from artists to writers.

Stalin had the ability to oversee purges, but he was showing more signs of poor health. His hands trembled. He drank too much and forced his associates to do the same. He smoked heavily and had insomnia.

On March 1, 1953, Stalin suffered a massive stroke. His daughter Svetlana and son Vasili were called to his bedside. Over the next few days, Svetlana held a vigil as Stalin grew worse. She said "he literally choked to death as we watched."

Stalin died on March 5, 1953. His body was placed in the mausoleum beside Lenin. His death brought an end to a murderous era that

COMMUNIST LEADERS FOLLOW THE CASKET OF JOSEPH STALIN, DURING THE LEADER'S FUNERAL IN 1953.

had begun with the Bolshevik revolution of 1917. Stalin's dictatorship cemented Communist rule in the Soviet Union and Eastern Europe for decades to come.

Rumors about Stalin's Death

JOSEPH STALIN'S DEATH WAS attributed to heart disease, but rumors circulated for years that he was poisoned. According to some reports, on the night of March 1, 1953, Stalin held one of his many all-night dinners with Politburo members, including Beria and Khrushchev. Afterward, Stalin was found unconscious on the floor of his bedroom. When Beria and the other diners learned of Stalin's illness, they assumed Stalin was drunk and sleeping off the effects of alcohol. Doctors did not arrive until the next morning, March 2. They diagnosed a massive stroke. But years later, after secret Soviet records were released for public viewing, some accounts appeared to support the possibility of poisoning. Doctors had found that Stalin was bleeding internally, which is not usual in a stroke. Some Russian historians and researchers suggest that, under orders from Beria, Stalin had been injected with a poison by one of his guards. No one will ever know for sure, because no witnesses are alive. But the rumors that Stalin was murdered live on.

CHAPTER 8

After Stalin

THE STALIN ERA WAS OVER in 1953, but communism was alive and well. After Stalin's death, Georgi Malenkov, Stalin's close comrade and deputy prime minister, became prime minister and also head of the Communist Party. From 1953 to 1955, Malenkov and Nikita Khrushchev struggled for power. In late 1953, Khrushchev launched an attack on Malenkov's long-time ally, Beria. Malenkov had appointed Beria first deputy prime minister and reappointed him head of the secret police. With Khrushchev encouraging the attacks, Beria was accused of treason, terrorism, and other crimes and was executed in December 1953.

By 1955 Khrushchev had replaced Malenkov as Communist Party chairman. Khrushchev firmly believed in communism but immediately began to make changes in the Soviet system and reduced Stalin's terror tactics. In 1956 he gave a speech to a closed session of the

Twentieth Party Congress in which he denounced Stalin, calling him a murderer and a tyrant. No Soviet leader had ever dared to make such accusations, even though most knew them to be true. It was the beginning of a period of reform called de-Stalinization.

Khrushchev made a variety of changes in Stalin's policies, such as releasing political prisoners, closing some labor camps, and relaxing censorship of the media. Reforms took place in agriculture and industry as well. Peasants were encouraged to grow more crops on their private plots. The government increased payments for crops grown on collective farms. In the factories, managers were allowed more control than they had had previously.

NIKITA KHRUSHCHEV

Some Eastern European countries began to hope they could gain freedom from Soviet rule. In 1956 there were anti-Soviet demonstrations in Poland. Workers in Poland staged protests and rioted for higher pay and better working conditions. Khrushchev threatened to send in troops to put down the workers. But he changed his mind and allowed more freedom for Poland as long as the country stayed loyal to the Warsaw Pact.

In Hungary, students and intellectuals were encouraged by the Polish demonstrations and began their own protests. Hungary's premier Imre Nagy called for free elections. He wanted to withdraw Hungary from the Warsaw Pact. An angry Khrushchev sent Soviet troops to Hungary to remove Nagy from power and to crush the uprising.

Tensions Increase

In 1957, under Khrushchev's rule, the Soviet Union successfully launched *Sputnik I*, the world's first artificial space satellite and the first of a series of Soviet satellites. *Sputnik I* marked the start of the space age and the race between the United States and the Soviet Union to land a human on the moon. It also raised fears in the United States that if the Soviets could launch satellites, they could also launch ballistic missiles that could carry nuclear weapons from Europe to the United States.

FAST FACT

Sputnik I, THE WORLD'S FIRST ARTIFICIAL SATELLITE, WAS ABOUT THE SIZE OF A BEACH BALL, 22.8 INCHES (58 CENTIMETERS) IN DIAMETER, AND WEIGHED ONLY 184 POUNDS (83.6 KILOGRAMS). IT TOOK ABOUT NINETY-EIGHT MINUTES TO ORBIT EARTH.

Khrushchev attempted to ease tensions with the West and talked about cooperation between the United States and the Soviet Union. That talk angered some Communists in the Soviet Union and other countries. Mao Zedong, for example, accused Khrushchev of discarding communist principles. Mao believed that the Soviets were becoming too friendly with the West. This was the beginning of a split between Communist China and the Soviet Union.

Sometimes Khrushchev showed that he could be tough when dealing with the West. For example, in 1961 he approved the construction of the Berlin Wall. The wall divided the Communist eastern section of the German city from the western section.

One of the most alarming threats was Khrushchev's 1962 decision to place nuclear missiles in Cuba, only 90 miles (145 km) from Florida. The missiles were aimed at the United States, creating the

Who Is the Leader of the World's Communists?

WHEN STALIN DIED IN 1953, China's Communist dictator Mao Zedong believed he should have become the leader of international Communism. But Soviet leader Nikita Khrushchev did not share that view, and he sneered at Mao's admiration of Stalin.

Cuban Missile Crisis, which prompted U.S. president John F. Kennedy to order a blockade of Cuba. Tensions mounted on both sides until Khrushchev agreed to withdraw the missiles in exchange for U.S. withdrawal of missiles from bases in Turkey. The incident was seen as a fiasco in the Soviet Union and around the world, and it helped diminish Khrushchev's stature as a leader.

Nevertheless, Khrushchev continued to promote a policy of peaceful coexistence between communists and capitalists. In 1963 he signed the Limited Nuclear Test Ban Treaty, in which the governments of the United States, Great Britain, and the Soviet Union agreed "to prohibit, to prevent, and not to carry out any nuclear weapon test explosion, or any other nuclear explosion, at any place under its jurisdiction or control."

Most historians agree that Khrushchev tried to follow two conflicting policies at the same time: cooperating with the West and attempting to intimidate Western nations. That, along with failing agricultural and industrial programs, helped lead to his forced retirement in 1964. With Khrushchev out of power, there was less emphasis on de-Stalinization and more emphasis on Soviet military strength.

The buildup of the military in the Soviet Union was a concern for Western nations, including the United States. During the 1960s, the Cold War had become a "hot war" in Vietnam, which shares a border with China. Like Korea, Vietnam had been divided between a Communist north and non-Communist south. U.S. troops assisted the South Vietnamese in their fight against the North, while Communist China and the Soviet Union supported the North Vietnamese.

The Soviet Union sent troops not only to assist North Vietnam but also to advance the spread of communism. For years the Soviet government denied that Soviet soldiers were involved. "It was only after the regime collapsed in 1991 that officials admitted more than 3,000 Soviet troops fought against the Americans in Vietnam," according to a news report on the radio program *Russia Today*.

During the 1970s, the Soviet government under Leonid I. Brezhnev continued to increase the size of its military. Brezhnev also supported Marxist revolutionary governments not only in Vietnam, but also in countries such as Angola, Mozambique, Somalia, Ethiopia, Grenada, and Nicaragua.

SALT Agreements

In 1972 U.S. president Richard Nixon met with Brezhnev, and the two signed the Strategic Arms Limitation Talks (SALT) agreement, which was meant to slow the nuclear arms race. Each nation agreed to set up only two antiballistic missile (missiles that intercept and destroy other missiles) sites and not to build any more intercontinental ballistic missiles. While the treaty helped establish a period of détente (easing of tensions) between the two countries, that détente ended in 1979 when the Soviets invaded Afghanistan, which borders the Soviet Union and Iran. As a result, the

United States Congress refused to ratify a second SALT agreement, refused to sell grain to the Soviet Union, and led sixty-one other nations in a boycott of Moscow's summer Olympic Games in 1980.

By 1990 Mikhail Gorbachev, who had been elected general secretary of the Communist Party in 1985, was the first president of the USSR. He had established some economic and social changes that he called perestroika (restructuring) and glasnost (openness). He encouraged freedom of expression, released some dissidents from prison, and signed the SALT agreement with the United States. Although he believed in central planning of the economy, he allowed some private enterprise in the USSR. He ended the occupation of Afghanistan, and in 1988 he told leaders of Warsaw Pact countries that the USSR would no longer interfere in their governments. This encouraged revolutionaries in these republics to overthrow Communist governments.

These examples of new freedom encouraged the USSR republics to press for their national identities and form fifteen republics independent of the USSR. These states formed regional organizations, one of which is the Commonwealth of Independent States. This includes all the former Soviet-controlled states except Estonia, Latvia, Lithuania, and Turkmenistan.

With the loss of its republics, the Soviet Union itself dissolved in 1991, and the Communist dictatorship was abolished. A Russian Federation formed, led by an elected president. The first freely elected president was Boris Yeltsin. He is remembered for his defiant stance against the control of the Communist Party and also for the failing economic conditions in his country. Before the end of his second term, Yeltsin made a surprise announcement that he was resigning. He chose Vladimir Putin to be the acting president until the next elections were held in 2000. Putin won the office that year.

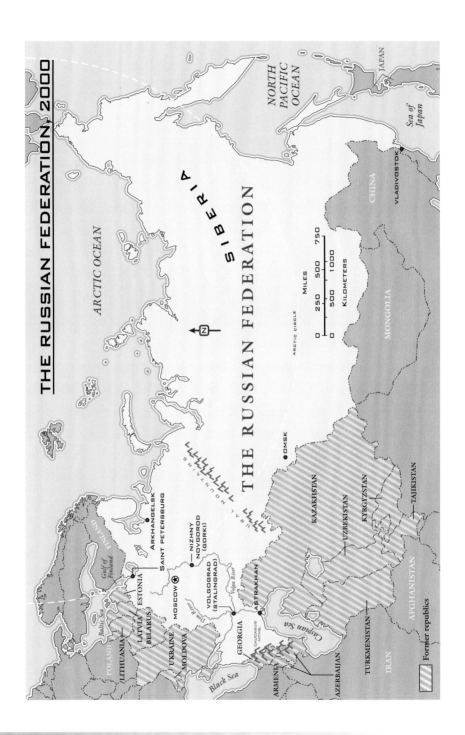

THE RUSSIAN FEDERATION, 2000

THE RUSSIAN FEDERATION

SIBERIA

ARCTIC OCEAN

NORTH PACIFIC OCEAN

Sea of Japan

JAPAN

CHINA

VLADIVOSTOK

MONGOLIA

ARCTIC CIRCLE

MILES

0 250 500 750

KILOMETERS

0 500 1000

OMSK

KAZAKHSTAN

UZBEKISTAN

KYRGYZSTAN

TAJIKISTAN

AFGHANISTAN

TURKMENISTAN

IRAN

AZERBAIJAN

ARMENIA

GEORGIA

CAUCASUS MTNS.

Caspian Sea

ASTRAKHAN

VOLGOGRAD (STALINGRAD)

Volga River

Don River

MOSCOW

Black Sea

MOLDOVA

UKRAINE

BELARUS

LATVIA

ESTONIA

LITHUANIA

POLAND

FINLAND

Gulf of Finland

Baltic Sea

SAINT PETERSBURG

NIZHNY NOVGOROD (GORKI)

ARKHANGELSK

URAL MOUNTAINS

N

Former republics

Toward the Future

In 2001 U.S. president George W. Bush met with Putin in Slovenia. During a news conference, Bush declared that he looked Putin in the eye and "found him to be very straightforward and trustworthy. . . . I was able to get a sense of his soul; a man deeply committed to his country and the best interests of his country."

However, at that time, some Russians expressed their unease with Putin, and over the next few years, he became increasingly dictatorial. He censored the media, ordered the arrest of political opponents, and initiated other repressive measures. He also charged the United States with imperialism. On numerous occasions, he criticized Bush for his attempts to establish a missile defense system in Eastern Europe in defiance of the SALT agreements.

In spite of Putin's autocratic ways, many Russians have been happy with the stable government. Since Putin's election, they have been enjoying a better life than under previous presidents and rulers. According to *Time* magazine, which chose Putin as its person of the year in 2007:

When historians talk about Putin's place in Russian history, they draw parallels with Stalin or the Tsars [czars]. Putin, one can't stress enough, is not a Stalin. There are no mass purges in Russia today, no broad climate of terror. But Putin is reconstituting a strong state . . . he is set to see out the rest of the drama of Russia's re-emergence. And almost no one in Russia is in a position to stop him. If he succeeds, Russia will become a political competitor to the U.S. and to rising nations like China and India. It will be one of the great powers of the new world.

Because of term limits, Putin's presidency ended in 2008. Putin picked his protégé, Dmitry Medvedev, to succeed him. With little competition, Medvedev was elected. At age forty-two, he is the youngest head of state since the rule of the czars. (When Lenin took over the government, he was forty-seven years old.) Medvedev named Putin prime minister, splitting the executive power between them. This, some observers say, may signal the kind of power shared briefly by Lenin and Stalin in the 1920s. But as a Russian journalist Julia Latynina wrote in 2008, "make no mistake, it is Putin's Russia." She noted, "In the West, people read that Putin has restored Russia's power and strengthened the ruling hierarchy. This is the image that the PR [public relations] agencies he has hired are trying to project. There may not be democracy in Putin's Russia, they say, but there is order."

For decades Russia had a single, strong ruler, and regardless of shared power, no one can be sure how far Putin—with the help of his protégé—will go. Some dissidents have talked about another revolution to destroy Putin's authoritarian control of the political process.

The Russian Revolution overthrew centuries of rule by a czar who inherited the title. In its place, the Russian people were ruled by a series of dictators, who also controlled much of Eastern Europe. Stalin's push to industrialize the Soviet Union caused misery for much of the country, as it forced the nation into the modern world. The suppression of freedom and rights under the Communist dictators continued a land of people unused to democracy. It will be up to future generations to decide whether the Russian Federation will follow the path of democracy or of authoritarian rule.

Timeline

1905	Protestors against the czar are massacred. The Imperial Army crushes the revolt that follows. Czar Nicholas II signs October Manifesto that establishes legislature (Duma).
1914	World War I begins. Russia suffers heavy losses.
1915	Czar Nicholas II takes charge of the Imperial Army.
1917	The Bolshevik Revolution begins. Czar Nicholas II abdicates. Vladimir Lenin leads the Bolshiviks, who stage a coup.
1918	The Brest-Litovsk Treaty is signed. Constituent Assembly dissolved. Civil War between Reds and Whites breaks out. Leon Trotsky is appointed Commissar (minister) of War. The Declaration of Rights of the Working and Exploited People bans private ownership of land.
1919	Comintern, an international organization, is founded to spread communism worldwide.
1920	Anarchists Emma Goldman and Alexander Berkman arrive in Russia. Civil War ends.
1921	Lenin establishes a New Economic Policy that eases the 1918 nationalization of industry and markets and allows the sale of some goods in the private market. Sailors and soldiers at the naval fortress on the island of Kronstadt rebel. Goldman and Berkman leave Russia.
1921–1922	A severe famine kills millions of Russians.

1922	Georgia, Armenia, and Azerbaijan form the Transcaucasian Soviet Federated Socialist Republic. Bolshevik leader Vladimir Lenin suffers several strokes.
1924	Lenin dies. A struggle for Communist leadership begins.
1925	The Communist Central Committee forces Trotsky to give up his post as war commissar.
1927	The Central Committee forces Trotsky out of the Communist Party.
1928	Joseph Stalin becomes leader of the Soviet Union and ends the New Economic Policy. He establishes his five-year collectivization plan.
1934	Stalin initiates a purge of the Leningrad Soviet. Stalin and his secret police conspire to murder Sergei Kirov, a member of the Politburo and Stalin's friend.
1936–1938	Stalin conducts a series of show trials of perceived enemies who were forced to confess publicly.
1939	Stalin's and Hitler's representatives sign the Nazi-Soviet Pact. Germany invades Poland. Soviet forces move into Poland to occupy its eastern half, according to the terms of the secret portion of the Nazi-Soviet Pact. World War II begins.
1940	Germany, Italy, and Japan form a World War II alliance known as the Axis.
1941	Germany begins a military assault on the Soviet Union. U.S. president Franklin Roosevelt sends aid to the Soviets. The Japanese bomb Pearl Harbor, and the United States enters World War II.
1943	Stalin meets with Roosevelt and British prime minister Winston Churchill in Tehran, Iran.

1944	Stalin appoints Lavrenti Beria, head of the secret police, as supervisor of the USSR's atomic energy project.
1945	Stalin, Roosevelt, and Churchill meet at Yalta, in southern Russia, to discuss how to divide Germany once the Nazis surrender. U.S. president Harry Truman orders a war plane to drop atomic bombs on Hiroshima and Nagasaki, Japan. World War II ends.
1947	The USSR installs Communist regimes in countries of Eastern Europe. A cold war between Communist countries, especially the Soviet Union, and Western nations begins.
1948	The Soviets set up a blockade, barring food and other necessities from reaching West Berlin. The United States, Great Britain, and France airlift supplies into Berlin, and the Soviets lift the blockade in 1949.
1949	Non-Communist Western nations form a military alliance, the North Atlantic Treaty Organization (NATO). The Soviet Union tests its first atomic bomb.
1950	Stalin and China's Communist leader Mao Zedong sign a Treaty of Friendship, Alliance, and Mutual Assistance. Stalin supports the North Korean invasion of South Korea, which results in war. The United Nations (UN), an organization to promote international cooperation, backs South Korea.
1953	Stalin dies. Nikita Khrushchev gains power within the Communist Party.
1955	The Soviets create the Warsaw Pact, a mutual defense treaty between the USSR and Eastern European countries. Khrushchev becomes Communist Party chairman.
1956	Khrushchev gives a speech condemning Stalin.

1957	The Soviet Union successfully launches *Sputnik I*. A space race between the Soviet Union and the United States begins.
1960	A nuclear arms race begins, with Communist countries competing against Western nations for superiority in production and stockpiles of nuclear weapons.
1961	The United States becomes involved in the Vietnam War.
1962	U.S. president John F. Kennedy learns the Soviets have secretly built military bases with nuclear weapons in Cuba. He orders a naval blockade of the island, bringing the United States and the Soviet Union close to nuclear war. A secret treaty ends standoff.
1979	The Soviet Union invades Afghanistan. The United States boycotts the 1980 Olympics in Moscow.
1985	Mikhail Gorbachev heads the Soviet Union. Reforms include glasnost (openness) and perestroika (restructuring).
1989	The fall of the Berlin Wall. Eastern Warsaw Pact nations overthrow Communist governments and form republics.
1991	The Soviet Union dissolves, and an independent Russian Federation forms. Russia's first freely elected president, Boris Yeltsin, takes office.
1999	Yeltsin resigns, and Vladimir Putin becomes Russia's acting president.
2000	Putin is elected Russia's president.
2008	Putin does not seek election because of term limits. Dmitry Medvedev becomes president. He names Putin prime minister.

Glossary

anarchy: the complete freedom from any government

armistice: a temporary agreement ending fighting between opponents

Bolsheviks: a Russian political party that changed its name to the Communist Party in 1918

bourgeoisie: in communist theory, the middle class, made up of merchants and owners of small businesses

capitalism: an economic system based on private ownership of property, resources, and the means to produce and distribute goods

coalition: an alliance

cold war: a period of tension between countries, without actual military fighting

Comintern: an international organization founded in Russia in 1919 to spread communist ideas worldwide

communism: an economic system in which there is public ownership and government control of resources and the means to produce and distribute goods

czar: an emperor or monarch

czarina: the wife of a czar

democracy: a government in which the supreme power is vested in the people, who elect representatives to government

guerrillas: armed forces who are not part of a regular military but engage in hit-and-run warfare in small units

hemophilia: a potentially life-threatening blood disease in which the blood does not clot

militia: a citizen army rather than a professional military force

monarchy: a government ruled by a monarch—a king, queen, or emperor—who inherits the title

Politburo: political bureau of the Communist Party's Central Committee in the Soviet Union

proletariat: in communist theory, workers or the working class

provisional government: a temporary government

regent: a person who rules when the official ruler is a child, is ill, or is absent

republic: a nation in which the citizens are entitled to vote for government officials; the head of state is usually a president

socialism: a number of different economic and political theories that call for government ownership of means of production and distribution of goods

Socialist Revolutionary Party: a political party in Russia that believed peasants, not industrial workers, would lead the revolution

soviets: councils that acted like governing bodies at local, regional, and national levels in the USSR

Who's Who?

Svetlana Alliluyeva (Stalina) (1926–): The only daughter of Joseph Stalin and his second wife, Nadezhda Alliluyeva, Svetlana was the couple's youngest child. With her family, Svetlana spent her early childhood in an apartment in the Kremlin and on the weekends in a dacha outside Moscow. Her care was primarily the responsibility of a nanny whom she dearly loved and stayed with for years. Cooks, maids, and a governess also made sure all of her needs were fulfilled. Svetlana reported that her childhood was happy, and she fondly recalled summers at the dacha where she joined her mother and an aunt in walks to hunt wild berries, mushrooms, and nuts.

Svetlana was only six when her mother died. She did not learn until she was a teenager that Nadya had committed suicide. After Nadya's death, the family and servants moved to another apartment in a Moscow building that also contained Stalin's office. Svetlana was sent to school for the first time at the age of seven. She enjoyed studying and learned several languages.

While a teenager, Svetlana became estranged from her father when she began to learn about Stalin's brutal treatment of relatives and family friends. In 1943 Svetlana enrolled at the University of Moscow, where she earned a doctorate in Russian literature. She met and married a fellow Moscow University student, Grigori Morozov. The two had a son, Joseph, in 1945. The couple divorced in 1947. She married again in 1949 and had a daughter, Eketrina, in 1950. That marriage ended in divorce that same year.

After Stalin's death, Svetlana took her mother's maiden name, Alliluyeva. In 1963 she established a relationship with Brajesh Singh, a visiting member of the Indian Communist Party, but Singh was gravely ill and died in 1965. Svetlana took his ashes to his family in India and stayed in the Singh home.

In 1967 Svetlana left India for the United States and there denounced Stalin and the Soviets, creating public outrage in the USSR. Svetlana's autobiographical book *Twenty Letters to a Friend* was published, which was critical of the Soviets and added to the USSR's outrage. Her other published works include *Only One Year* and *Faraway Music*.

Svetlana married a noted American architect William Peters in 1970, and she took the name Lana Peters. The Peters had a daughter named Olga, but the couple broke up not long afterward. During the 1980s, Svetlana and Olga moved first to Great Britain, then to the Soviet Union, and back to the United States. At 82 years old in 2008, she is said to be living in a retirement home.

Lavrenti Beria (1899–1953): During the Stalin era in the Soviet Union, Lavrenti Beria was one of the most feared individuals connected with the Communist government. He was head of the secret police from 1938 to 1953.

Beria was born in Georgia, Stalin's homeland, during the time of the Russian Empire. He planned to be an architect, but after college graduation he became a building inspector. In 1917 he joined the Bolshevik Party. During the revolution, he organized a Bolshevik group in Georgia, which became part of the Soviet Union. By 1922 he was deputy head of the Georgian secret police. In 1924 Beria led the putdown of a nationalist uprising in Georgia and saw to the execution of an estimated ten thousand people. Because of his work in Georgia, Beria was awarded the Order of the Red Banner, a high military honor.

In 1938 Stalin appointed Beria head of the People's Commissariat of Internal Affairs, otherwise known as the NKVD, the Soviet security service. Beria was in charge of numerous purges of so-called enemies of the people and was responsible for millions of deaths.

Stalin appointed Beria to the USSR's atomic bomb project in 1944. Beria's secret police spied on the U.S. nuclear bomb program and gained technology that allowed the Soviet Union to build a nuclear bomb, which was tested in 1949. Part of Beria's responsibility for the USSR's bomb project was supplying the labor force. He ordered tens of thousands of prisoners from the Gulag to work in the uranium mines and uranium processing plants to produce uranium for the project. After 1946 he was a deputy prime minister, still in charge of foreign espionage and the nuclear bomb project.

After Stalin's death, Beria tried to gain enough power to become Stalin's successor. But he was foiled by Nikita Khrushchev, who accused him of treason, terrorism, and other crimes. Beria was executed in December 1953.

Emma Goldman (1869–1940): Born in the province of Kovno, Russia (modern Kaunas, Lithuania), Emma Goldman grew up in a poor Jewish family. Her parents were subject to the rule of Czar Alexander II. Goldman's father, Abraham, was an innkeeper, but he barely made a living. He treated Emma harshly, often beating her because she dared to argue with him and to express independent ideas or because she misbehaved at school.

When Goldman was sixteen years old, she fled to the United States to escape an arranged marriage. She lived for several years in Rochester, New York. In Rochester she met and married Jacob Kershner. They divorced, and Goldman moved to New York City in 1889.

In New York, Goldman met anarchists who had come from Europe. She became an anarchist, with the belief that people should live free of governments, which forced them to go to war or to work under inhuman conditions. To spread her views, Goldman became a passionate speaker and prolific writer. She was the most visible anarchist in the United States. The press called her the most dangerous woman in the country. Frequently, the police tried to ban Goldman's public appearances. She was arrested many times for violating police orders.

The U.S. immigration department eventually charged Goldman under the Anarchist Exclusion Act, which barred known anarchists from entering the country and allowed the deportation of known anarchists. In December 1919, the United States deported Goldman along with 248 others labeled as anarchists. She was sent to Russia, where she hoped to become part of the revolutionary movement. But she soon became disillusioned and left Russia for exile in England, France, and Spain.

Maxim Gorky (1868–1936): Born in Nizhny Novgorod, Russia, Maxim Gorky was named Aleksey Maximovich Peshkov at birth. He attended school until he was eight years old, when his grandfather forced him to be an apprentice (trainee) with various tradesmen. He ran away from home at the age of twelve, barely surviving by working odd jobs. It was such a desperate time that he began using the name Maxim Gorky, which means "the bitter one" in Russian.

With the help of one employer, he learned to read. Literature became his passion and shaped his own career as a major literary figure in Russia.

Gorky's first collection of short stories, *Sketches and Stories*, was published in 1898. The book was so successful that Gorky became one of the most popular writers in the country. His published works include novels, short stories, and plays that deal with realistic portrayals of peasant and worker life.

Gorky supported the revolution of 1917 and was a good friend of Vladimir Lenin, founder of the Bolshevik Party and revolutionary leader. But he became disillusioned with the Communist regime and left Russia in 1921.

At the invitation of Communist dictator Joseph Stalin, Gorky returned to Russia in 1928 and became a Stalin supporter. He published literature that gave an optimistic presentation of socialist reality and glorified revolutionary ideals. Gorky was the first president of the Union of Soviet Writers, founded in 1932. He died in 1936, but the cause of his death is not certain. Some accounts say he died of pneumonia or heart disease. Others say he was poisoned on Stalin's orders.

Nikita Sergeyevich Khrushchev (1894–1971): Born in a mud hut in Kalinova, Ukraine, Nikita Khrushchev was the son of a coal miner. He was reared among peasant farmers and miners and had only a brief elementary education. During his early teenage years, he worked as a miner and pipefitter for a coal mining company. He was not drafted in World War I, because he was needed as a factory worker.

In 1917 Khrushchev became involved in workers' organizations. During the Russian Civil War, he joined the Bolshevik Party. He fought with the Red Army against the anti-Communist White Army. Khrushchev's wife, Galina, was one of thousands who died from famine during the extreme food shortages.

In 1922 the Communist Party sent Khrushchev to a secondary school, where he finished his education and became a political organizer. At the school he met Nina Petrovna, who became his second wife, in 1924.

Throughout the 1930s, Khrushchev steadily rose within the Communist Party. He became first secretary of the Moscow branch of the party in 1935 and first secretary of the Ukrainian branch of the party in 1938. He played a prominent role in Stalin's purges of the late 1930s. In 1939 Khrushchev became a member of the Communist Party's Politburo.

During World War II, Stalin made him a political officer in the army. After Stalin died in 1953, Khrushchev engaged in a struggle to become head of the Communist Party. He won that post in 1955 and in 1956 began a policy of de-Stalinization, denouncing Stalin's brutal tactics and beginning a series of agricultural and industrial reforms. He also attempted to ease tensions between the Soviet Union and the United States. But his reforms failed, and his dealings with the United States and the West were sometimes peaceful and sometimes threatening.

Communist Party members forced him to retire in 1964. Before he died in 1971, Khrushchev dictated his memoirs, which were eventually published in three books, the last one in 1990.

Vladimir Ilyich Lenin (1870–1924): Vladimir Ilyich Ulyanov, later known as Vladimir Lenin, was born in Simbirsk (modern-day Ulyanovsk), east of Moscow, on the Volga River. His father was an inspector of schools in Simbirsk.

In 1887 Lenin's brother Alexander was arrested and hanged for his part in a plot to assassinate the czar. The whole Ulyanov family became outcasts, and Lenin was barred from Saint Petersburg University. He instead enrolled in the law school at Kazan University, which his father had attended. During his first year, he was expelled for attending a protest against university conditions. He spent the next few years reading Marxist literature and studying law on his own. In 1891 he was given permission to take the law exams and passed them easily.

In 1893 he moved to Saint Petersburg (later renamed Petrograd). There he organized the League for the Liberation of the Working Class. As a result of his activities, he was arrested in 1897, along with other leaders of the organization, including Nadezhda Krupskaya, who would later become his wife. Lenin spent fifteen months in jail and then was exiled for three years to Siberia, where he and Krupskaya were married.

After his exile in Siberia ended, Lenin spent many years in European countries, organizing a revolutionary movement. He returned to Russia during the failed 1905 revolution, then fled to Switzerland. He continued his activities through an underground organization.

Lenin returned to Russia again in 1917. The Germans allowed a train to pass through Germany with Lenin aboard, and he arrived in Petrograd a month after the February Revolution. In Petrograd, Lenin, with Leon Trotsky, organized the 1917 Bolshevik October Revolution.

Lenin and the Red Army were soon involved in the Russian Civil War, fighting the anti-Bolshevik White Army. After the Reds defeated the Whites, Lenin's power increased. He ruled the Soviet Union as a dictator until his death in 1924.

Nestor Ivanovich Makhno (1889–1935): Nestor Makhno was one of seven children born to a poor peasant family in the Ukrainian village of Gulyai-Polye. His father died when he was less than a year old, and his mother reared all the children. Because of the family's extreme poverty, Makhno went to work as a shepherd at the age of seven. He received only four years of schooling and at age twelve began work as a farmhand for wealthy landowners.

During his teenage years, Makhno became interested in anarchism. He was arrested in 1908 for anarchist activities. In prison he met Peter Arshinov, a leading anarchist who was jailed for smuggling anarchist literature into Russia. Arshinov, older and better educated, taught Makhno basic anarchist doctrine.

In 1917 Russia's Provisional Government granted official pardons to political prisoners, including Makhno. After he was released, he returned to his home village to build an anarchist movement and to lead peasants in seizing land from gentry in the region. He also organized the Revolutionary Insurgent Army of the Ukraine, a guerrilla force frequently called the Makhnovists. Makhno claimed that his insurgents were the only revolutionaries true to the cause of workers and peasants.

During the Russian Civil War, the Bolshevik Red Army enlisted the support of the Makhnovists in its fight against the White Army. As the Reds increasingly won battles in the Civil War, they turned on Makhno's insurgents, killing many officers and arresting members of anarchist organizations. Makhno himself was nearly captured at his headquarters in Gulyai-Polye, but he escaped with only a leg wound. In 1921 Makhno fled to Paris, France. He was in exile when he died in 1935.

Karl Marx (1818–1883): A German philosopher, Karl Marx, along with his long-time collaborator Friedrich Engels, established the theory of communism that was followed by Vladimir Lenin, leader of the Bolshevik Party in Russia.

Marx was born in Trier, Germany, a city on the Mosel River. His parents, Hirschel and Henrietta Marx, were Jews but joined a Protestant church to avoid anti-Semitic persecution. His father was a lawyer, and Marx studied law, history, and philosophy in Bonn and Berlin, Germany. After earning his doctorate, Marx edited a radical newspaper, in which he pointed out the terrible working conditions in factories and criticized wealthy landowners who exploited peasants. Because of his views, he was forced to resign from the paper.

Marx left Germany and moved with his wife, Jenny von Westphalen, to Paris, France, in 1844. There he met Engels. The two collaborated on *The Communist Manifesto*, a blueprint for revolution that was published in 1848. They argued that throughout history, people who control the land and means of production amass wealth and power, while the proletariat remains powerless. They predicted that the proletariat would revolt against the ruling class and bring about a classless society and an economic system known as communism.

A number of European countries faced revolutions in 1848, and Marx hoped that the working class would succeed. But the revolts failed. Marx was convinced that the proletariat had to develop revolutionary political parties in order to triumph. He spent decades trying to spread his ideas through socialist organizations and with his writings, including *Das Kapital*, which was about capitalism. This work and many of his other writings created controversy before his death in 1883. People continue to read and study his ideas.

Nicholas Alexandrovich Romanov (1868–1918): Nicholas II was the last czar of the Russian Empire. He was born in Tsarskoe Selo, south of St. Petersburg, where the imperial palace was located. He was the son of Czar Alexander III and Czarina Marie Fedorovna of Russia. Nicholas's parents provided him with an excellent education and prepared him to be czar. But because of his sheltered life, he grew up not knowing how most people in the empire lived and not understanding the economic and social problems of the country.

Nicholas II married a German princess, Alexandra of Hesse. After his father's death in 1894, Nicholas and Alexandra were crowned czar and czarina.

In 1904 Russia went to war with Japan over who would control trading and investing rights in Manchuria, in China's far northeastern corner. Manchuria was rich with raw materials needed for industry, such as timber, coal, and iron. In 1905 Japan defeated Russia. Russians blamed Nicholas II for the loss.

In 1905 a workers' demonstration, protesting long hours and low wages, was crushed by Nicholas's Imperial Army. During World War I, Russia suffered so many defeats in the summer of 1915 that Nicholas went to the front to take control of the army. But the soldiers were poorly trained and lacked adequate equipment. They frequently were forced to retreat.

Widespread discontent and threats of revolt across Russia forced Nicholas to abdicate in 1917. Lenin placed him and his family under house arrest at Tsarskoe Selo. Months later they were moved to Ekaterinburg, east of the Ural Mountains, and placed under guard in a private home. The entire family was executed in 1918.

Joseph Stalin (1879–1953): Born in Gori, Georgia, Iosif Vissarionovich Dzhugashvili, later Joseph Stalin, was one of four children. His three siblings died, and he was in poor health during his childhood. Although his parents were poor, his mother was able to enroll him in a religious school, where he did well in his studies. However, he was expelled because he tried to convince other students to accept socialism.

While a young man, he changed his name to Stalin, because it means "Man of Steel." Stalin became a member of the Social Democratic Labor Party in 1901 and organized strikes and resistance to the czar. He was arrested, imprisoned, and sent to Siberia. He escaped and continued his organizing. He was imprisoned and escaped four more times.

Leon Trotsky (1879–1940): At birth, Leon Trotsky was named Lev Davidovich Bronstein. His Jewish family lived in Yanovka, Ukraine, then part of Russia, where they were fairly successful farmers. In his autobiography, Trotsky described his early years:

> My childhood does not appear to me like a sunny meadow, as it does to the small minority; neither does it appear like a

dark cave of hunger, violence and misery, as it does to the majority. Mine was the grayish childhood of a lower-middle-class family, spent in a village in an obscure corner where nature is wide, and manners, views and interests are pinched and narrow.

Trotsky received his education at Odessa, a Ukrainian port city on the Black Sea. As a teenager, he learned about Karl Marx's theory of socialism. He became involved in an underground workers' union. In 1898 he was arrested for revolutionary activities and jailed, the first of many imprisonments. He was exiled to Siberia in 1900 and escaped in 1902. Using a fake passport with the name Trotsky, he eventually went to London, England, where he joined the Social Democratic Party. In London he worked with Vladimir Lenin on a revolutionary journal.

Trotsky returned to Russia during the 1905 revolution and became chairman of the Saint Petersburg Soviet. The czar crushed the revolution, and Trotsky was arrested again. He was again exiled to Siberia. While in prison there, he developed his theories about a revolution that would spread worldwide.

Trotsky again escaped from Siberia and over the next decade lived in various countries. He settled in New York City in January 1917 but returned to Russia after the overthrow of Czar Nicholas II. He was one of the chief organizers, along with Lenin, of the October Revolution. He held several positions with the Bolshevik government, including Commissar of War in 1918. He led the Red Army during the Russian Civil War.

After Lenin's death in 1924, Trotsky competed with Stalin for party leadership. Stalin eventually sent Trotsky into exile, first in Turkey, then in France and Norway. Trotsky and his family found refuge in Mexico, where he was murdered in 1940, possibly on orders from Stalin.

Source Notes

8   Sheila Fitzpatrick and Yuri Slezkine, eds., *In the Shadow of the Revolution: Life Stories of Russian Women from 1917 to the Second World War* (Princeton, NJ: Princeton University Press, 2000), 34.

10   Richard Pipes, *A Concise History of the Russian Revolution* (New York: Vintage Books, 1995), 77.

10   Francis A. March and Richard J. Beamish, *History of the World War: An Authentic Narrative of the World's Greatest War* (Project Gutenberg, 2006), http://www.gutenberg.org/etext/18993, 428, also available online at Steven Kreis, "The Russian Revolution, February–October 1917," *The History Guide*, October 11, 2006, http://www.historyguide.org/europe/lecture5.html (November 26, 2007).

11   Orlando Figes, *A People's Tragedy: The Russian Revolution, 1891–1924* (New York: Penguin Books, 1996), 173.

11   Konstantin Ivanovich Globachev, "Report of the Chief of the Petrograd Okhranka, Major-General Globachev, to the Ministry of Internal Affairs on Events in the Capital, 26 February 1917," *History of the Soviet Union*, 2002, http://www.uea.ac.uk/his/webcours/russia/documents/globchev.shtml (November 26, 2007).

12   Eduard M. Dune, *Notes of a Red Guard*, eds. and trans. Diane P. Koenker and S. A. Smith (Urbana: University of Illinois Press, 1993), 32.

18   V. I. Lenin, *Lenin Collected Works* (Moscow: Progress Publishers, 1964), 38–41.

18   Ibid.

19   Figes, 364.

20   V. I. Lenin, "To Our Comrades in War-Prisoner Camps," (leaflet, March 1917), *Lenin Collected Works* (Moscow: Progress Publishers, 1964, 343.

22   Mary Antin, *The Promised Land*, 8–9 (Project Gutenberg, 2007), http://www.gutenberg.org/files/20885/20885-h/20885-h.htm (February 25, 2008).

23   Leon Trotsky, "Vodka, the Church, and the Cinema," *Pravda*, July 12, 1923, February 5, 2007, http://www.marx.org/archive/trotsky/women/life/23_07_12.htm (September 1, 2008).

24   Leon Trotsky, "Lenin: Forming the Government," *Marxists Internet Archive*, April 14, 2007, http://www.marxists.org/archive/trotsky/1925/lenin/06.htm (March 7, 2008).

25–26 V. I. Lenin, *Collected Works*, 423–425, *From Marx to Mao*, December 1999, http://www.marx2mao.com/Lenin/DRWP18.html (December 17, 2007).

27   V. I. Lenin, "Note to F. E. Dzerzhinsky, December 7, 1917," *Lenin Collected Works*, 374–376, *Marxists Internet Archive*, November 2000, http://www.marxists.org/archive/lenin/works/1917/dec/07.htm (March 7, 2008).

27–28 Fitzpatrick and Slezkine, 86.

28–29 Anna Horsbrugh-Porter, ed., with interviews by Elena Snow and Frances Welch, "Eugenia Peacock," *Memories of Revolution: Russian Women Remember* (London: Routledge, 1993), 108.

29   Figes, 529.

30–31 V. I. Lenin, "The Socialist Fatherland Is in Danger!" *Lenin Collected Works*, 30–33, *Marxists Internet Archives*, March 2002, http://www.marxists.org/archive/lenin/works/1918/feb/21b.htm (December 18, 2007).

33   Nestor Makhno, "The Anarchist Revolution," *The Nestor Makhno Archive*, n.d., http://www.nestormakhno.info/english/anar_rev.htm (December 22, 2007).

33   W. Bruce Lincoln, *Red Victory: A History of the Russian Civil War* (New York: Da Capo Press, 1999), 326.

34   Peter Arshinov, *History of the Makhnovist Movement, 1918–1921*, trans. Lorraine Perlman and Fredy Perlman (Detroit: Black & Red, 1923; Chicago: Solidarity, 1974), 47.

34   Ibid., 56.

36   John Reed, "Preface," *Ten Days That Shook the World* (New York: Boni & Liveright, 1922), 13.

41   Fitzpatrick and Slezkine, 120.

41–42 Dune, 124.

42–43 Victor Serge, *Revolution in Danger: Writings from Russia, 1919/1920*, trans. Ian Birchall (London: Redwords, 1997), 11.

43   Harold Williams, "Denikin Moves Capital to Rostov," *New York Times*, September 19, 1919. n.d., http://query.nytimes.com/mem/ archive-free/pdf?_r=1&res=9E00E3DE123AE03ABC4A51DFBF66 8382609EDE&oref=slogin (January 10, 2008).

43   Serge, 64.

44   V. I. Lenin, "All Out for the Fight Against Denikin!" *Lenin Collected Works*, 436–455, *Marxists Internet Archives*, n.d., http://marxists .anu.edu.au/archive/lenin/works/1919/jul/03.htm#i (January 2, 2008).

46   Serge, 11.

47   Figes, 618.

48–49 Horsbrugh-Porter, 42–43.

49   United States Holocaust Memorial Museum, "Pogroms," *Holocaust Encyclopedia*, October 25, 2007, http://www.ushmm .org/wlc/article.php?lang=en&ModuleId=10005183 (February 25, 2008).

52   Emma Goldman, *Living My Life* (1931; repr., New York: Knopf, 1970), 743.

53   Michiko Kakutani, "Books of the Times; From a Rebel to a Pen of Bolshevism," *New York Times*, June 16, 1989, http://query.nytimes .com/gst/fullpage.html?res=950DE7D71E3DF935A25755C0A96F 948260&sec=&spon=&pagewanted=all (September 1, 2008).

54   Alexander Berkman, *The Kronstadt Rebellion*, March 18, 2000, available online at *Anarchy Archives*, n.d., http://dwardmac.pitzer.edu/ anarchist_archives/bright/berkman/kronstadt/berkkron.html (January 16, 2008).

55–56 Alexander Berkman, *The Bolshevik Myth*, 303, February 3, 2001, available online at *Anarchy Archives*, n.d., http://dwardmac.pitzer.edu/ anarchist_archives/bright/berkman/bmyth/bmch38.html (January 16, 2008).

56   Alexander Berkman, *The Bolshevik Myth*, 318, February 3, 2001, available online at *Anarchy Archives*, n.d., http://dwardmac.pitzer.edu/Anarchist _Archives/bright/berkman/bmyth/bmch39.html#4 (January 19, 2008).

56–57 Goldman, 927.

57   Leon Trotsky, *The Revolution Betrayed*, 1936, *Marxists Internet Archives*, April 22, 2007, http://www.marxists.org/archive/ trotsky/1936/revbet/ch02.htm (January 17, 2008).

58   Nikolai Bukharin, "Economic Organization in Soviet Russia," *The Living Age*, July–September 1922, 2006, http://www.marxists.org/ archive/bukharin/works/1922/economic-organisation.htm (January 17, 2008).

60 "Famine Years," *The German Colonies on the Volga River*, n.d., http://www.volgagermans.net/volgagermans/Volga%20Famine%20Years.htm (January 18, 2008).

60 Dune, 175.

61–62 *New York Times*, "Russia Must Free Captives to Get Aid," n.d., http://query.nytimes.com/mem/archive-free/pdf?_r=2&res=9F0DE5D817 31EF33A25756C2A9619C946095D6CF&oref=slogin&oref=slogin (January 19, 2008).

63 "Kellogg Confirms Reports of Famine," *New York Times*, October 24, 1921, 7.

65–66 Lenin, V. I., "Lenin's Letter to Congress, dictated December 25, 1922," *Marxists Internet Archives*, n.d., http://www.marxists.org/archive/lenin/works/1922/dec/testamnt/congress.htm (January 20, 2008).

66 Lenin, V. I., "Lenin's Addition to the Letter to Congress, Dictated January 4, 1923," *Marxists Internet Archives*, n.d., http://www.marxists.org/archive/lenin/works/1922/dec/testamnt/congress.htm (January 20, 2008).

68 Robert Conquest, *Stalin: Breaker of Nations* (New York: Viking Penguin, 1991), 111.

68 J. V. Stalin, "On the Death of Lenin, a Speech Delivered at the Second All-Union Congress of Soviets," August 2004, http://www.marxists.org/reference/archive/stalin/works/1924/01/30.htm (January 23, 2008).

69 Ibid.

69 Serge Schmemann, "Soviet Disarray; Preserving Lenin, the High-Tech Icon," *New York Times*, December 17, 1991, http://query.nytimes.com/gst/fullpage.html?res=9D0CEED7113BF934A25751C1A967958260 (February 22, 2008).

70 Robert Conquest, 111.

72 MIA, "Socialism in One Country," *Encyclopedia of Marxism*, n.d., http://www.marxists.org/glossary/terms/s/o.htm (February 21, 2008).

73 In Defence of Marxism, "Testament of Leon Trotsky," February 27, 1940, *Trotsky.net*, n.d., http://www.trotsky.net/trotsky_year/political_testament.html (September 1, 2008).

74 J. V. Stalin, "On the Grain Front," *Works*, vol. 11, 88, May 1, 1997, http://www.marx2mao.com/PDFs/StWorks11.pdf (January 28, 2008).

74 Conquest, 159.

74 J. V. Stalin, *Works*, vol. 12, 173, May 1, 1997, http://www.marx2mao.com/PDFs/StWorks12.pdf (January 28, 2008).

75 Fitzpatrick and Slezkine, 223.

76 J. V. Stalin, *Works*, vol. 13 (Moscow: Foreign Languages Publishing House, 1954), 41.

77 PBS, "Interview with Tatiana Fedorova, Soviet Construction Worker," *People's Century*, PBS Online, April 20, 1998, http://www.pbs.org/wgbh/peoplescentury/episodes/redflag/fedorovatranscript.html (February 21, 2008).

77–78 Mary M. Leder, *My Life in Stalinist Russia: An American Woman Looks Back*, ed. Lauri Bernstein (Bloomington: Indiana University Press, 2001), 25.

78 Ibid., 299.

80 Jonathan Lewis and Phillip Whitehead, *Stalin: A Time for Judgement* (New York: Pantheon Books, 1990), 65–66.

81 Rosamond Richardson, *Stalin's Shadow: Inside the Family of One of the*

World's Greatest Tyrants (New York: St. Martin's Press, 1993), 124, 126.

84   Nikita Khrushchev, Khrushchev Remembers: The Glasnost Tapes, trans. and ed., Jerrold L. Schecter and Vyacheslav V. Luchkov (New York: Little Brown, 1990), 24–25.

86   Aleksandr Solzhenitsyn, The Gulag Archipelago, 1918–1956, authorized abridgment (New York: Harper, 2002), 321.

86   Lewis and Whitehead, 91.

86   Ibid., 97.

88   University of North Carolina, "Letter from Rykov, March 13, 1938," ibiblio.org, n.d., http://www.ibiblio.org/expo/soviet.exhibit/a2rykov.html (February 6, 2008).

88   PBS, Red Files, PBS Online, 1999, http://www.pbs.org/redfiles/prop/deep/prop_deep_ref_detail.htm (May 15, 2008).

89   Conquest, 212.

90   PBS. "Interview with Tatiana Fedorova, Soviet Construction Worker"

90–91   Steven Kreis, "Stalin and the Cult of Personality," The History Guide: Lectures on Twentieth Century Europe, 2004, http://www.historyguide.org/europe/cult.html#first (February 8, 2008).

91   J. V. Stalin, "Letter to Comrade Choumiatsky," Works, vol. 14, May 1, 1997, http://www.marx2mao.com/PDFs/StWorks14.pdf (February 8, 2008).

92   A. O. Avidenko, "Hymn to Stalin," Modern History Source Book, n.d., http://www.fordham.edu/halsall/mod/stalin-worship.html (February 9, 2008).

92   Vagif Samadoghlu, "Stalin's Personality Cult: Three Times I Changed My Mind," *Azerbaijan International*, Autumn 1999, http://azer

.com/aiweb/categories/magazine/73_folder/73_articles/73_stalin .html (February 11, 2008).

93   Will Bennett, "How Shaw Defended Stalin's Mass Killings," *Telegraph.com*, June 18, 2003, http://www.telegraph.co.uk/news/ main.jhtml?xml=/news/2003/06/18/nshaw18.xml&sSheet=/ news/2003/06/18/ixhome.html (February 12, 2008).

95   Mao Zedong, "On the People's Democratic Dictatorship—in Commemoration of the 28th Anniversary of the Communist Party of China, June 30, 1949," *Selected Works*, vol. 5 (New York: International Publishers, n.d.), 423.

96   "Nazi-Soviet Pact," *Spartacus Educationa*, n.d., http://www .spartacus.schoolnet.co.uk/RUSnazipact.htm (February 14, 2008).

98   Paul Halsall, ed., "Text of the Nazi-Soviet Non-Aggression Pact, Article I," *Modern History Sourcebook*, n.d., http://www.fordham .edu/halsall/mod/modsbook.html (February 14, 2008).

98   Alan Bullock, *Hitler and Stalin: Parallel Lives* (New York: Vintage Books, 1993), 611.

100   Richardson, 164.

101   Khrushchev, 56.

101   Ibid., 57.

103   Ibis Communications, "The Siege of Leningrad, 1941–1944," *EyeWitness to History*, 2006, http://www.eyewitnesstohistory.com (February 18, 2008).

105   Richardson, 170–171.

107 Edvard Radzinsky, *Stalin: The First In-Depth Biography Based on Explosive New Documents from Russia's Secret Archives,* trans. H. T. Willetts (New York: Doubleday, 1996), 520.

107–108 Winston S. Churchill, "The Sinews of Peace (Iron Curtain)," (speech, Westminster College, Fulton, MO, March 5, 1946), *The Churchill Centre,* n.d., http://www.winstonchurchill.org/i4a/pages/index .cfm?pageid=429 (February 19, 2008).

110 Khrushchev, 70–71.

112 Ibid., 66.

113 Conquest, 312.

118 U.S. Department of State, "Treaty Banning Nuclear Weapon Tests in the Atmosphere, in Outer Space and Under Water," *USA.gov,* n.d., http://www.state.gov/t/ac/trt/4797.htm (March 1, 2008).

119 TV-Novosti, "USSR 'Secret' Vietnam Soldiers Speak Out," *Russia Today,* February 16, 2008, http://www.russiatoday.ru/news/ news/21019 (March 4, 2008).

122 Office of the Press Secretary, "Press Conference by President Bush and Russian Federation President Putin," June 16, 2001, http:// www.whitehouse.gov/news/releases/2001/06/20010618.html (June 21, 2008).

122 Adi Ignatius, with reporting by Yuri Zarakhovich and Dario Thuburn, "A Tsar Is Born," *Time,* December 4, 2007, http:// www.time.com/time/specials/2007/personoftheyear/article/ 1,28804,1690753_1690757_1690766,00.html (March 2, 2008).

123 Julia Latynina, "Life in Putin's Russia," *Washington Post,* June 22, 2008, B01.

137 Leon Trotsky, *My Life* (New York: Charles Scribners Sons, 1930), 1.

Bibliography

Ashinov, Peter. *History of the Makhnovist Movement 1918–1921*. Translated by Lorraine Perlman and Fredy Perlman. Berlin: The Group of German Anarchists. Reprint, Detroit: Black & Red, 1923; Chicago: Solidarity, 1974.

Bennett, Will. "How Shaw Defended Stalin's Mass Killings," *Telegraph.com*. June 18, 2003. http://www.telegraph.co.uk/news/main.jhtml?xml=/news/2003/06/18/nshaw18.xml&sSheet=/news/2003/06/18/ixhome.html (February 12, 2008).

Berkman, Alexander. *The Bolshevik Myth*. February 3, 2001. http://dwardmac.pitzer.edu/anarchist_archives/bright/berkman/bmyth/bmch38.html (August 28, 2008).

———. *The Kronstadt Rebellion*. Berlin: Der Sindikalist, 1922.

Bukharin, Nikolai. "Economic Organization in Soviet Russia." *The Living Age*. 2006. http://www.marxists.org/archive/bukharin/works/1922/economic-organisation.htm (January 17, 2008).

Churchill, Winston S. "The Sinews of Peace (Iron Curtain)." Speech given at Westminster College, Fulton, Missouri, March 5, 1946. N.d. http://www.winstonchurchill.org/i4a/pages/index.cfm?pageid=429 (February 19, 2008).

Conquest, Robert. *Stalin: Breaker of Nations*. New York: Viking Penguin, 1991.

Dune, Eduard M. *Notes of a Red Guard*. Edited and translated by Diane P. Koenker and S. A. Smith. Urbana: University of Illinois Press, 1993.

"Famine Years." *The German Colonies on the Volga River*. N.d. http://www.volgagermans.net/volgagermans/Volga%20Famine%20Years.htm (January 18, 2008).

Fedorova, Tatiana. "Interview with Tatiana Fedorova, Soviet Construction Worker." *People's Century, PBS Online*, April 20, 1998. www.pbs.

org/wgbh/peoplescentury/episodes/redflag/fedorovatranscript.html (February 21, 2008).

Figes, Orlando. *A People's Tragedy: The Russian Revolution, 1891–1924.* New York: Penguin Books, 1996.

Fitzpatrick, Sheila, and Yuri Slezkine, eds. *In the Shadow of the Revolution: Life Stories of Russian Women from 1917 to the Second World War.* Princeton, NJ: Princeton University Press, 2000.

Gay, Kathlyn, and Martin Gay. *Encyclopedia of Political Anarchy.* Santa Barbara, CA: ABC-CLIO, 1999.

———. *The Importance of Emma Goldman.* San Diego, CA: Lucent Books, 1997.

Globachev, Konstantin Ivanovich. "Report of the Chief of the Petrograd Okhranka, Major-General Globachev, to the Ministry of Internal Affairs on Events in the Capital, 26 February 1917." *History of the Soviet Union.* 2002. http://www.uea.ac.uk/his/webcours/russia/documents/globchev.shtml (November 26, 2007).

Goldman, Emma. *Living My Life.* 1931. Reprint, New York: Knopf, 1970.

Horsbrugh-Porter, Anna. ed., with Elena Snow and Frances Welch, interviewers. *Memories of Revolution: Russian Women Remember.* London: Routledge, 1993.

Ignatius, Adi, with reporting by Yuri Zarakhovich and Dario Thuburn. "A Tsar Is Born." *Time,* December 4, 2007. http://www.time.com/time/specials/2007/personoftheyear/article/1,28804,1690753_1690757_1690766,00.html (March 2, 2008).

Khrushchev, Nikita. *Khrushchev Remembers: The Glasnost Tapes.* Translated and edited by Jerrold L. Schecter, with Vyacheslav V. Luchkov. New York: Little Brown, 1990.

Kreis, Steven. "The Russian Revolution, February–October 1917." October 11, 2006. http://www.historyguide.org/europe/lecture5.html (November 26, 2007).

————. "Stalin and the Cult of Personality." *The History Guide: Lectures on Twentieth Century Europe*. May 13, 2004. http://www.historyguide.org/europe/cult.html#first (February 8, 2008).

Leder, Mary M. My *Life in Stalinist Russia: An American Woman Looks Back*. Edited by Lauri Bernstein. Bloomington and Indianapolis: Indiana University Press, 2001.

Lenin, V. I. *Lenin Collected Works*. Moscow: Progress Publishers, 1972.

————."Lenin's Addition to the Letter to Congress, Dictated January 4, 1923." N.d. http://www.marxists.org/archive/lenin/works/1922/dec/testamnt/congress.htm (January 20, 2008).

————. "Lenin's Letter to Congress, Dictated December 25, 1922." N.d. http://www.marxists.org/archive/lenin/works/1922/dec/testamnt/congress.htm (January 20, 2008).

Lewis, Jonathan, and Phillip Whitehead. *Stalin: A Time for Judgement*. New York: Pantheon Books, 1990.

Lincoln, W. Bruce. *Red Victory: A History of the Russian Civil War*. New York: Da Capo Press, 1999.

Makhno, Nestor. "The Anarchist Revolution." *The Nestor Makhno Archive*. N.d. http://www.nestormakhno.info/english/anar_rev.htm (December 22, 2007).

March, Francis A., in collaboration with Richard J. Beamish. *History of the World War: An Authentic Narrative of the World's Greatest War*. Philadelphia and Chicago: United Publishers, 1919. Project Gutenberg Ebook. August 6, 2006. http://www.gutenberg.org/etext/18993 (August 28, 2008).

"Nazi-Soviet Non-Aggression Pact, Article I." *Modern History Sourcebook*. 1997. http://www.fordham.edu/halsall/mod/modsbook.html (February 14, 2008).

Pipes, Richard. *A Concise History of the Russian Revolution*. New York: Vintage Books/Random House, 1995.

Radzinsky, Edvard. *Stalin: The First In-Depth Biography Based on Explosive New*

Documents from Russia's Secret Archives. Translated by H. T. Willetts. New York: Doubleday, 1996.

Richardson, Rosamond. *Stalin's Shadow: Inside the Family of One of the World's Greatest Tyrants.* New York: St. Martin's Press, 1993.

"Russia Must Free Captives to Get Aid." *New York Times.* July 25, 1921. http://query.nytimes.com/mem/archive-free/pdf?_r=2&res=9F0DE5D81731E F33A25756C2A9619C946095D6CF&oref=slogin&oref=slogin (January 19, 2008).

Samadoghlu, Vagif. "Stalin's Personality Cult: Three Times I Changed My Mind." *Azerbaijan International,* Autumn 1999. http://azer.com/aiweb/categories/magazine/73_folder/73_articles/73_stalin.html (February 11, 2008).

Serge, Victor. *Revolution in Danger: Writings from Russia, 1919/1920.* Translated by Ian Birchall. London: Redwords, 1997.

Service, Robert. *Stalin: A Biography.* Cambridge: The Belknap Press of Harvard University Press, 2005.

Solzhenitsyn, Aleksandr. *The Gulag Archipelago, 1918–1956,* Authorized Abridgment. New York: Harper, 2002.

Stalin, J. V. "Letter to Comrade Choumiatsky." *Works, Vol. 14.* N.d. http://www.marx2mao.com/PDFs/StWorks14.pdf (February 8, 2008).

———. "On the Death of Lenin, a Speech Delivered at the Second All-Union Congress of Soviets," August 2004. http://www.marxists.org/reference/archive/stalin/works/1924/01/30.htm (January 23, 2008).

———. *Works, Vol. 12.* N.d. http://www.marx2mao.com/PDFs/StWorks12.pdf (March 12, 2008).

———. *Works, Vol. 13.* 1954. N.d. http://www.marx2mao.com/PDFs/StWorks13.pdf (January 31, 2008).

Trotsky, Leon. "Lenin: Forming the Government." 1925. April 14, 2007. http://www.marxists.org/archive/trotsky/1925/lenin/06.htm (March 7, 2008).

———. "On the Suppressed Testament of Lenin." December 1932. April 24, 2007. http://www.marxists.org/archive/trotsky/1932/12/lenin.htm (January 26, 2008)

———. *The Revolution Betrayed.* 1936. April 22, 2007. http://www.marxists .org/archive/trotsky/1936/revbet/ch02.htm (January 17, 2008).

U.S. Department of State. *Treaty Banning Nuclear Weapon Tests in the Atmosphere, in Outer Space and Under Water.*, Signed at Moscow August 5, 1963. N.d. http://www.state.gov/t/ac/trt/4797.htm (March 1, 2008).

"USSR 'Secret' Vietnam Soldiers Speak Out." *Russia Today.* February 16, 2008. http://www.russiatoday.ru/news/news/21019 (March 4, 2008).

Williams, Harold. "Denikin Moves Capital to Rostov." *New York Times,* September 19, 1919. <http://query.nytimes.com/mem/archive-free/pdf ?_r=1&res=9E00E3DE123AE03ABC4A51DFBF668382609EDE&oref =slogin (January 10, 2008).

For Further Reading and Websites

BOOKS

Appignanesi, Oscar. *Introducing Lenin and the Russian Revolution*. New York: Totem Books, 2000.

Fitzpatrick, Sheila. *The Russian Revolution*. Oxford and New York: Oxford University Press, 2008.

Goldstein, Margaret J. *V. I. Lenin*. Minneapolis: Twenty-First Century Books, 2007.

Márquez, Herón. *Russia in Pictures*. Minneapolis: Twenty-First Century Books, 2004.

Smith, Stephen A. *The Russian Revolution: A Very Short Introduction*. Oxford University Press, 2002.

Streissguth, Tom. *Vladimir Putin*. Minneapolis: Twenty-First Century Books, 2005.

Zuehlke, Jeffrey. *Joseph Stalin*. Minneapolis: Twenty-First Century Books, 2006.

WEBSITES

Country Studies. "Russia."
http://lcweb2.loc.gov/frd/cs/rutoc.html
This Library of Congress Federal Research Division website has a section on Russia. Chapter 2 covers the years 1917 to1991, which includes the revolutions, the Civil War, New Economic Policy, Stalin's rise to power, purges and terror, and leaders who followed Stalin.

Internet Modern History Sourcebook: Russian Revolution
http://www.fordham.edu/halsall/mod/modsbook39.html
This site provides sections on the czarist empire, the Russian Revolution, Bolshevik rule in 1924, and Stalinism. Links within each section cover a variety of topics on the revolution and its aftermath.

J. V. Stalin Internet Library
http://www.marx2mao.com/Stalin/Index.html
This site consists of fourteen volumes of Joseph Stalin's writings, from 1901 to 1940.

Lenin Internet Archive
http://www.marxists.org/archive/lenin/index.htm
Vladimir Lenin's written works are the main part of this website. It also contains numerous photographs and a biography of Lenin.

The Leon Trotsky Internet Archive
http://www.marxists.org/archive/trotsky/index.htm
Trotsky's writings from 1901 to 1940 are on this website. There are also photographs of Trotsky, biographies, and Trotsky's autobiography, *My Life.*

Index

Photo Acknowledgments

The images in this book are used with the permission of: © Laura Westlund/ Independent Picture Service, pp. 6, 111, 121; © Image Asset Management Ltd./ SuperStock, p. 7; © UnderwoodArchives.com, p. 17; © The Print Collector/Alamy, p. 21; © Photo12/The Image Works, p. 29; The Art Archive/Imperial War Museum, p. 38; © Scherl/Sueddeutsche Zeitung Photo/The Image Works, p. 45; The Granger Collection, New York, p. 55; Library of Congress, p. 59 (LC-USZ62-95141); © Topical Press Agency/Hulton Archive/Getty Images, p. 62; © Haynes Archive/ Popperfoto/Getty Images, p. 64; © Albert Harlingue/Roger Viollet/Archive Photos/Getty Images, p. 79; © Snark/Art Resource, NY, p. 89; © Keystone/Hulton Archive/Getty Images, p. 97; AP Photo, p. 102; AP Photo/apn, p. 109; © Russian Look/North Wind Picture Archives, p. 113; AP Photo/Str, p. 116.

Front Cover: © Popperfoto/Getty Images.

About the Author

Kathlyn Gay is the author of more than 120 books, some written in collaboration with family members who are scattered from coast to coast. Her books focus on social and environmental issues, culture, history, health, communication, and sports. Her writing has covered a range of age levels, from first readers and science booklets to young adult and adult nonfiction. Gay's work has also appeared in encyclopedias, teacher manuals, and portions of textbooks. Among her other published works are hundreds of magazine features and stories; plays; and promotional materials.